LOUIS C. TIFFANY'S
ART GLASS

Also by Robert Koch

Louis C. Tiffany: Rebel in Glass

Louis C. Tiffany's Glass • Bronzes • Lamps.
A Complete Collector's Guide

LOUIS C. TIFFANY'S ART GLASS

ROBERT KOCH

CROWN PUBLISHERS, INC. NEW YORK

Inquiries should be addressed to Crown Publishers, Inc., One Park Avenue,
New York, N.Y. 10016

Printed in the United States of America

Published simultaneously in Canada by
General Publishing Company Limited

Graphic design Hans Thöni, Berne
American Edition Designed by Shari de Miskey

Library of Congress Cataloging in Publication Data

Koch, Robert, 1918–
Louis C. Tiffany's art glass.

Bibliography: p.
Includes index.

1. Tiffany, Louis Comfort, 1848–1933.   2. Glassware
—United States.   3. Decoration and ornament—Art
nouveau. I. Title.

NK5198.T5K6155 1977 748.2'913 77-3531
ISBN 0–517–53068–6

CONTENTS

Preface   ix
Introduction   1

1. PICTURE WINDOWS   3
2. ARTIFICIAL ILLUMINATION   7
3. GLASS OF THE NINETIES   9
4. VARIATIONS IN GLASS   19
5. COMMERCIAL GLASS AND OTHER PRODUCTS   25
6. COLLECTORS AND COLLECTIONS   29

Conclusion   33
Selected Statements by Louis C. Tiffany   35
Registry Numbers by Years   40
Select Bibliography   41
Notes   43
Photo Credits   45
Index   131

PREFACE

The idea for this volume originated with Paul Haupt, Berne, who felt there was a need for a book in German on Tiffany glass. The original intent was to extract from *Louis C. Tiffany: Rebel in Glass* and *Louis C. Tiffany's Glass—Bronzes—Lamps* to produce a German edition, but during the course of preparation this book emerged as a totally new concept, more a sequel than a repetition. Tiffany glass is seen here in a new light.

From the first, my concern with the career of Louis Comfort Tiffany has been to assess his contributions to the origins of modern art both at home and abroad. My first book, *Rebel in Glass* (Crown Publishers, Inc., 1964), was a biography that set down the facts of his life with a minimum of critical comment. My *Glass—Bronzes—Lamps* (Crown Publishers, Inc., 1971) was put together from original photographs and catalogs that serve as a collector's guide for products made in the workshops under Tiffany's direction. I depended on the contemporary comments of S. Bing to place the art of Tiffany in proper perspective. I also participated in the publication of an anthology of Bing's writings, which appeared as *Artistic America, Tiffany Glass and Art Nouveau* (Cambridge, Mass.: The M.I.T. Press, 1970). Bing was an astute critic who helped to promote the most progressive artists of his time.

The next problem was to define Art Nouveau and its importance to modern art. I had serious reservations about tracing it to the Impressionists or the Pre-Raphaelites until Robert Schmutzler's thesis traced the sources to William Blake. By 1880 Louis C. Tiffany was already familiar with the art of Blake through his friend and associate, the painter Elihu Vedder. Recent discoveries of some early examples of Tiffany's work helped to make this clear.

On Thanksgiving Day, November 1973, it was my good fortune to be able to acquire the glass panel that Tiffany designed and made for himself in 1880. It is both Art Nouveau and Abstract Expressionist, inspired by Blake and strikingly modern. Using this as a point of departure, all the glass produced later under Tiffany's direct supervision takes on a new significance.

The design and production of this book is entirely the work of Paul Haupt and his designer, Hans Thöni, in Berne. I express my gratitude to Glen Bailey, Joan Foran, and Beryl Smith for typing the manuscript, and to the several museum curators who provided me with captions. Above all, it was the advice and encouragement of my wife, Gladys, that made it possible for this work to be completed.

Robert Koch
South Norwalk, Connecticut

INTRODUCTION

As the biographer of Louis C. Tiffany (1848–1933), I found it a challenge to determine which of his many achievements have been the most significant. His work as a painter is relatively unknown and, in my opinion, underrated. Since his death there has been no exhibition devoted exclusively to his oils and watercolors, and the few that are in public collections or have come onto the market are mostly not representative of his best work. His descendants, from the five children who survived him, still possess and prize the bulk of his paintings. In his youth, Tiffany had been heralded as one of the most promising talents in America, but his interests in glass and decoration left him little time to paint. His early landscapes have a poetic quality comparable to the work of Corot and Inness, his scenes of North Africa show his decorative genius, and his later floral paintings are exuberant tributes to natural forms. He regretted never having studied figure drawing and felt himself inadequate in depicting human anatomy, but this did not prevent him from completing a few very strong oil paintings with figural subjects.

Tiffany, one of the first professional interior decorators, was often hampered by his wealthy clients. In this field his most successful accomplishments can be found in the three homes he planned for himself and his family, none of which is still intact. In other interiors, one has to identify the elements consistent with his personal style.

Here the artist emerges as a creator and an early exponent of the free creative energy and anticlassical naturalism associated with Art Nouveau. In the history of American decorative arts, Tiffany stood squarely between Henry H. Richardson and Louis Sullivan as an early exponent of the principles of modernism. A window that he created for his "Bella" apartment in 1880 is both high Art Nouveau and an example of abstract expressionism.

In his published writings, Tiffany lauds the superior quality of American glass and its uses in the arts, along with the importance of color in his quest for beauty in the natural world of forms. The writers he retained to promote him and his wares featured his desires to elevate the decorative arts to the level of the fine arts, but his contemporary American artists criticized him for being overly commercial. Only one man in his day, S. Bing, a dealer in Paris who was a native of Germany, saw Tiffany's highest achievement in the blown glass of the 1890s, a belief that was restated by Robert Schmutzler in 1962 and Mario Amaya in 1967.

Tiffany lived beyond the time of his importance to the arts, and so he witnessed the wane of his popularity. Even though he had been a daring innovator in his youth, he strongly condemned the experiments of the modernists of the early twentieth century. At the time of his death, during the Great Depression of the 1930s, the market was flooded with objects produced in his workshops. His private collection was sold at auction in 1946, when the market was still depressed.

The Tiffany revival went hand in hand with a renewed appreciation for the merits of Art Nouveau, and it was Tiffany's vases that first reflected this trend. The value of the unique pieces of Tiffany's glassware increased one hundred times in the two decades following the Second World War. Then, in the present decade, Tiffany lamps caught up with and surpassed the value of Tiffany vases. Fortunately the process has been a selective one, and more and more critics are coming to the conclusion that Bing was right, that Tiffany's art in the free-blown glass made in his furnaces was his greatest achievement, transcending the limitations of the style known as Art Nouveau and ascending to the highest levels of pure art.

It is hoped that the story and the illustrations in this volume will help reinforce this idea, and inspire future generations of craftsmen as Tiffany himself would have wished.

1   PICTURE WINDOWS

On November 1, 1865, Louis C. Tiffany, then only seventeen years of age, set sail from New York aboard the steamship *Scotia* for his first trip to Europe. Much to his father's dismay, he had already decided on a career in art. His itinerary included London, Paris, Nice, Rome, and Palermo, and the sketches that he made as a record of the trip proved his talent, but his family felt that art was not a respectable profession.[1]

His father, Charles Lewis Tiffany, was a very successful merchant in silver and jewelry who had made a great deal of money supplying the Union Army with swords and medals during the Civil War. He had hoped that his son would take an interest in the business of Tiffany and Company, but that was not to be. Young Louis rejected a formal education and spent his time with other young artists in the studio of landscape painter George Inness in New York. The watercolors that remain from his trip show him already interested in flowers (Ill. 32) and trees (Ill. 33), influenced by Inness and, indirectly, by Corot. He remained a romantic lover of nature for the rest of his life.

Louis C. Tiffany's success as a painter was assured before he reached thirty. His work was exhibited in Philadelphia in 1876 and in Paris at the Exposition of 1878. He was the youngest member of the National Academy of Design in New York. He then decided to experiment with glass as a medium for painting and for various uses in interior decoration. In 1879 he began to make stained-glass windows for the homes of some of his father's friends. One of these, a New York drug merchant named George Kemp, commissioned Tiffany to decorate his home on Fifth Avenue. For the dining room, Tiffany painted a frieze of fall fruit and, where the frieze was interrupted by transoms over two doors, he made panels of opalescent leaded glass that carried the same theme. One of these represents gourds, the other, eggplants. The glass is all handmade, of varying thickness and density; the lines of lead represent the plant stems.[2] With the glass left over from these Kemp dining-room panels, Tiffany made two windows for his own studio apartment, one essentially the same design as the eggplant panel in the Kemp dining room, the other totally abstract (Ills. 2 & 35).

Having observed this window of 1880 in an old photograph, Robert Schmutzler said of it that Tiffany had "suddenly hit upon a design that is pure High Art Nouveau. This manifests itself here, as in most cases, in a two-dimensional manner. The pattern on the window is entirely abstract and soft, it flows asymmetrically in the manner of veined marble . . . movement expressed in solidified glass." But the design of this window was no accident. Tiffany planned it on a clear glass window in his studio, using palette scrapings and thick paint. The source for the design, as in so

3

many other instances of emerging Art Nouveau, can be traced to the art of William Blake, as Schmutzler has correctly demonstrated. Tiffany had become familiar with Blake's works through his friend, the American symbolist painter, Elihu Vedder, who also supplied Tiffany with designs for his use in the same "Bella" apartment that housed the abstract window.[3]

George Kemp arranged for Tiffany to obtain the commission to decorate the Veterans Room of the Seventh Regiment Armory in New York. This was his first large-scale job in a public building, and here he collaborated with the architect Stanford White. Although the latter exerted a restraining influence on Tiffany, the completed interiors were an immediate success. They launched Tiffany on a new career that was to occupy him for more than a decade. In 1883, he and his associates were invited by President Chester Arthur to redecorate the White House in Washington. After this, his business expanded at such a rapid rate that he was forced to turn most of the designing over to his associates. In 1885, after the death of his first wife, Tiffany took a personal interest in two major projects, the decoration of the Lyceum Theatre and the construction of the Tiffany mansion, both in New York. Unfortunately neither of these is still extant.

In 1886, Tiffany remarried, this time the daughter of a Presbyterian minister, and he soon became increasingly involved with ecclesiastical windows and interiors.

In 1889, after dutifully being present at the birth of his eighth child, his last, Louis C. Tiffany left for Paris to visit the Universal Exposition. There two things impressed him greatly. The iridescent surfaces on some of the glass exhibited by the Austrian firm of Lobmeyer made him realize that the effects he had already achieved on tiles and windows could also be possible on blown glass. He also discovered that his foremost American rival, John La Farge, had on display a window of opalescent glass produced in the manner he had helped to develop. This window received much praise from the critics, and made Tiffany realize that he, too, could display and sell his windows in Europe.[4]

The opportunity to do this was made possible by S. Bing, who was then a dealer in Oriental art and the publisher of *Artistic Japan*.[5] In 1891, he arranged for several French artists to supply Tiffany with designs that could be used for windows (Ills. 3, 41, & 42). Ten such windows were made in Tiffany's studio in New York, and these were displayed in Paris at the *Salon du Champs de Mars* in 1894 and were also on view when S. Bing opened his *Salon de l'Art Nouveau* in 1895.[6]

For the Paris *Exposition Universelle* in 1900, Tiffany sent two very large windows (Ill. 43), one designed by his staff artist, Frederick Wilson, and the other, "Four Seasons," which he had designed himself (Ill. 40), He was then 52 years old, at the peak of his career, the most famous American artist, a leader in Art Nouveau, which had become an international style. Above all, at that time, he felt the need to perpetuate himself and his ideas, something that he could most successfully accomplish through the production of blown-glass objects that would have a worldwide distribution.

After 1900, most of the designing of Tiffany windows was done by staff artists retained for that purpose. Tiffany had reorganized his business in 1892, changing the name from Tiffany Glass Company to Tiffany Glass and Decoration Company, with a separately managed ecclesiastical department responsible for church windows, mosaics, and mausoleums. In 1900, the name was again changed, this time to Tiffany Studios. Artist-craftsmen were trained in the highly specialized techniques, and orders for memorials poured in from all over the country. By 1910, there were Tiffany windows installed in churches in forty states, the District of Columbia, Canada, Australia, England, Scotland, and France.[7] Even the secular works for important public buildings were created by designers commissioned for the particular job. Tiffany, as president of the firm, retained only the right of approval, and he exercised this without exception until his retirement in 1919. The production of church windows by Tiffany Studios continued until 1938, five years after Tiffany's death, when the firm was liquidated. Since then changing conditions, particularly in urban centers, have resulted in the demolition of many church buildings that once housed Tiffany windows, and in the process the windows too were lost. In New York City alone more than one half the windows originally produced by Tiffany Studios have been destroyed. Only a small fraction have been acquired by public or private collectors, but fortunately some of these are the finest examples.

2 ❧ ARTIFICIAL ILLUMINATION

Louis C. Tiffany is reputed to have said that his lamps were a by-product of his work with windows, but this is not true in the literal sense. He first became involved with the use of glass and artificial light while decorating the Lyceum Theatre in New York in 1885. Here Thomas A. Edison, the inventor, himself installed the first electric footlights ever used for a stage, and the sconces, designed and installed by Tiffany, were described by a contemporary critic as "like fire in monster emeralds" and "the electric light from the clustered globes pendant from the ceiling is soft and pleasantly diffused."[8] A watercolor by Tiffany's hand in the Metropolitan Museum of Art (Ill. 45), incorporating a self-portrait of the artist enthroned, shows his concept of the interior of this theatre. A large hanging fixture of about the same date (Ill. 46) is perhaps the oldest Tiffany glass lighting device still extant. Its metalwork clearly derives from early medieval sources in a manner that also anticipates the achievements of several prominent Art Nouveau designers.

Not until 1896 were portable lamps made by Tiffany and available for sale to the public. The first were student lamps, kerosene burning, made according to patents of 1876 and 1879, for which Tiffany obtained the parts ready-made; he finished these with his own formulas for decorating and providing a surface patina, and added iridescent glass shades. Next he made lamps with blown-glass bases and shades, and the following year he acquired a bronze foundry to manufacture a variety of bases, candlesticks, and other objects so that he did not need to depend on other makers. By 1900, as seen in his Paris exhibition (Ill. 87), his furnaces were producing a large variety of objects of metal and glass, none of which closely resembles the windows made for the same World's Fair.

In 1898, Tiffany introduced his first lamp that combined a metal standard with a leaded glass shade made in the manner that he had perfected for use in windows. It was an immediate success, and within a decade his studios were producing lampshades from designs based on a wide variety of plants and flowers (Ills. 47–52). The Tiffany Studios price list of 1906 itemizes more than 400 oil and electric lamps and hanging shades, each one a different model. This list also shows over 150 different candlesticks and candle lamps and nearly 300 other objects useful for office and home. Each of these bears a model number and is priced for retail sale.[9] In the next decade, up to the outbreak of the First World War, Tiffany's inventory was still further expanded. All these items were in addition to the blown glass.

Tiffany Studios produced, besides, many items for special order. The design for one of these (Ill. 53) shows a hanging shade intended for a palace in Berne, Switzerland, approved with the autograph of Louis C. Tiffany.

At the peak of production, about 1905, Tiffany Studios employed nearly 200 craftsmen. According to S. Bing:

Tiffany saw only one means of effecting this perfect union between the various branches of industry: the establishment of a large factory, a vast central workshop that would consolidate under one roof an army of craftsmen representing every relevant technique; glassmakers and stone setters, silversmiths, embroiderers and weavers, casemakers and carvers, gilders, jewelers, cabinetmakers—all working to give shape to the carefully planned concepts of a group of directing artists, themselves united by a common current of ideas.[10]

The guiding principle underlying all the diverse articles produced by this large group of artisans was that they should be inspired by natural forms. Lamps not only were to be works of art but in many cases were conceived as flowers in bloom, day and night, winter and summer. Desk sets were made in designs resembling pine needles, grape vines (Ill. 54), and in Byzantine, Ottonian, Islamic, and Chinese interlace patterns that provide a linear animation of surfaces. Tiffany's love of nature, his association with Art Nouveau, and his admiration for non-Western sources are apparent in every object produced under his direction.

Another principle strictly adhered to at Tiffany Studios was to maintain the highest quality regardless of cost. Only the finest bronze was used as the basic metal for lamp bases, candlesticks, and desk sets. Glass lampshades were assembled using copper foil and bronze solder, to make them far more durable than those leaded in the traditional manner. Every part was hand finished and carefully fitted with the precision of a finely tooled instrument. Tiffany developed a pride in craftsmanship in every one of his employees. No shortcuts or economies were allowed while Tiffany himself was supervising the work.

Tiffany lamps were, when they were new—and they are still today—the finest quality electric lighting devices ever made. They were and still are the most expensive. It is impossible to determine how many were made or how many are still in existence, but the stories of how many have been destroyed are greatly exaggerated. The name Tiffany became a generic name for all lamps and fixtures using leaded glass, and the genuine articles rapidly became confused with the products of the dozens of imitators who produced a cheaper and therefore less durable line of similar items.

The factory mark "Tiffany Studios, New York" and the model number were usually stamped in the metal or applied in the form of a metal tag on articles intended for retail sale. This "signature" was often omitted—considered unnecessary on unique or commissioned articles. As with other works of art, the authenticity of Tiffany objects can best be determined from style and technique.

In 1891, Arthur J. Nash came to the United States and met Louis C. Tiffany. Nash had been a manager of the Edward Webb Glasshouse in the Stourbridge district in England; he came to America to visit his brother and to serve as a sales representative for English glass. At the time that they met, Tiffany was planning an elaborate chapel for display at the World's Columbian Exposition, to be held in Chicago in 1893. He convinced Nash to stay in America and help him establish a furnace for glassblowing, and the two formed a partnership named The Stourbridge Glass Company. In February 1892, they purchased a structure in Corona, Long Island, that had been erected as a laundry and cleaning establishment.[11]

Arthur Nash had no experience at blowing glass. Tiffany knew more than Nash, as he had handled a blowpipe and had made and worked with window glass for more than twelve years. As the Sandwich Glass Company in Massachusetts had gone out of business in 1888, there were many glassblowers seeking employment, and Tiffany was already known as a generous employer. The first glassblower they hired was Thomas Manderson of Philadelphia. He had formerly been employed by Gillinder Brothers, whose glass had been exhibited at the Philadelphia Centennial Exposition in 1876, and who had been producing cameo glass since 1880. Manderson selected his own assistants, including his son William, John Hollingsworth, and George Parker. Martin Bach, an Alsatian

trained in the Saint Louis glasshouse, was hired as the mixer, and the ovens were turned on; the first glass they made was called Corona Glass. It was their first job to provide Tiffany with ornaments of blown glass for use in his Chicago chapel.

Arthur Nash, who was only one year younger than Tiffany, felt that their partnership should be an equal one. It remained so for only nine months. One night in the winter of 1892 the building burned to the ground and the night watchman lost his life in the fire. In order to build a bigger and better new furnace, Nash was forced to give up part of his shares to his partner, and the name of the plant was changed to Tiffany Furnaces, a subdivision of the Tiffany Glass Company, later becoming the Tiffany Glass and Decorating Company.

During the first nine months at Corona, the most important achievement was the creation of the "flower-form" vase. At first Nash urged the men to create traditionally shaped vases, emphasizing variety of decorations and color, but Tiffany encouraged them to be freer by rejecting almost all their finished products with the often repeated expression, "Too much Stourbridge!" It was only when Thomas Manderson completed the first tall stem vase in the shape of a tulip that Tiffany was truly pleased.

Achieving the proper iridescence on the surface of blown glass was a major problem for the first two years. The methods that Tiffany had been using to achieve a high and brilliant iridescence on his window and mosaic glass were only partly successful with blown glass. Window glass has a lime base whereas blown glass has a lead base, so new formulas were needed. Tiffany consulted five chemists until he found one who came up with the right answers. That was Dr. Parker McIlhenny of Philadelphia, who was immediately put on the Tiffany payroll. James Stewart, recalling the event in 1966, described it as follows:

I was there the day that we hit the colors. . . . I was sent down to the office to bring Mr. Tiffany up to show him this new vase that he never saw before. When he came up he was so delighted—I can see him prancing and dancing around there yet.[12]

The term "Favrile" was coined in February 1892 as a Tiffany trademark. As a word, it had nothing to do with the color or the iridescence. Originally Nash had suggested and used the spelling "Fabrile," a word deriving from old English, meaning pertaining to the craftsman or his craft. On September 26, 1894, the Tiffany Glass and Decorating Company filed the Favrile trademark to apply to all its manufactured products, including all kinds of glass, metals, and other materials. It was usually used redundantly with Tiffany's name as in "Tiffany Favrile Glass" or "Tiffany Favrile

Pottery" or "L. C. Tiffany Favrile."

One of the earliest recorded sales of a piece of Tiffany glass was on June 2, 1894, when the Musée des Arts Décoratifs in Paris purchased a green marbleized bowl with random gold threads from S. Bing (Ill. 59). Two more were acquired the same way in 1895 (Ills. 60 & 61), two in 1896, and one in 1899. In 1907, Tiffany presented the Musée with a collection of thirty-one pieces of his glassware so that they would have a representative group.

In New York Mr. and Mrs. Henry O. Havemeyer were Tiffany's first patrons for his free-blown glass hollow ware. In 1890, Tiffany had been in charge of the decoration of the Havemeyer house, so he easily convinced the Havemeyers to acquire a collection of his vases for themselves, and in 1896 they also volunteered to donate a group to the Metropolitan Museum of Art (Ills. 62–67). The first public viewings of the new line of Tiffany glass were opened simultaneously in December 1895 at S. Bing's first show at his *Salon de l'Art Nouveau* in Paris and at Tiffany's Fourth Avenue showrooms in New York. *The New York Times* called the glass "curious and entirely novel, both in color and texture." The following year, 1896, most of the pieces in this first New York show were acquired by the Smithsonian Institution in Washington, D.C. (Ills. 68–80). Another group was purchased by the Cincinnati Museum in 1897 (Ills. 6–9).

All these examples that are clearly documented

from the first five years of the production of Tiffany glass have only one element in common. That is the free-form quality of either their shape or their decoration. Glasses of varying colors and densities were blown and decorated so that the lines or veins of color expressed the character and structure of the material. Glass is worked as an aqueous mass and hardened from its molten state; the decoration was applied to accentuate its character. Tiffany's blown glass is the logical outgrowth of his experiments with tiles and windows in the 1880s. Other than the flower form of vase, the shapes of these vases and bowls almost defy classification. As stated in a Tiffany brochure of 1898, "The forms of Tiffany Favrile Glass are very largely derived from natural motives." The only alterations to the surfaces were either by polishing or by intaglio carving, to intensify the color or character of the glass.

At first the techniques were very simple. Clear, green, or amber bottle glass was the basis for the products of the first two years. Made in crude furnaces fired by a mixture of oil and steam, the early glass is full of impurities and bubbles. In 1895 the quality of the glass was greatly improved, and a second "shop" was added under the direction of George J. Cook.

Cook's specialties were different from those of Manderson. It was Cook who—under Tiffany's careful supervision—developed peacock, Cyp-riote, and lava glass, and also introduced the gooseneck or rosewater sprinkler shape. Cook remained at Tiffany's only until 1909, at which time the production of his special types of glass was terminated.

Peacock glass was achieved by combining five different types of glass, two of which were aventurine. The effect was that of feathers of iridescent blues and greens into which an opalescent "eye" could be inserted. One of the most successful of these is part of the Havemeyer gift of 1896 to the Metropolitan Museum of Art (Ill. 64). The gooseneck shape, often made of peacock glass, derives from a sixteenth-century Persian ritual rosewater sprinkler in the Edward C. Moore Collection (Moore, a silversmith, was a partner in Tiffany and Company until his death in 1892), then also in the Metropolitan Museum of Art. Louis C. Tiffany was certainly familiar with the Moore collection of Islamic glass; he derived several of his forms from it. Both Moore and Tiffany were also collectors of Japanese decorative arts.

Objects owned by the Metropolitan Museum of Art also inspired another kind of glass made for Tiffany by George Cook. A General De Cesnold had organized an archaeological dig on Cyprus in the hope of finding Aegean treasures. They succeeded in excavating a large selection of partly decomposed Roman glass, which was brought back to New York and admired for its rough surfaces and its iridescent colors. Thus Tiffany adopted the name "Cypriote" for the Tiffany glass that looks most like the ancient pieces that had been buried for centuries. Most often it has a rough irregular surface on a simple shape.

The freest and most abstract of all Tiffany glass is known as lava glass because of its resemblance to volcanic lava. This was one of Tiffany's favorites, but as it was not then popular, very few pieces were made. Most of these have uneven shapes, surfaces even rougher than Cypriote, and heavy applied glass either partly or wholly fused into the form. Added bosses or globs of glass sometimes give an added interest to the scheme of these pieces. Because of its daringly modern character, lava glass is most highly prized by collectors.

A third shop, also organized in the 1890s under James H. Grady of Sandwich, Massachusetts, was formed for the purpose of making and using millefiori canes. Grady's style is characterized by the lily pad and vine decoration that became the most popular of all the forms of decoration. It is interesting to note that at about the same time the painter Claude Monet also began to be fascinated with the pond lily.

Grady's shop made canes of all sizes, which were then imbedded in the bodies of vases and bowls and blown to create a new kind of overall decoration in various colors. From this came the "paperweight technique" that involved adding a casing of clear glass over the millefiori effects. A fourth shop under Arthur E. Saunders was added in 1900 because of the extensive demand for this type of glass. (Its contributions will be covered in the next chapter.)

Physically the Tiffany furnaces were constructed with sixteen glass pots grouped under eight arches, two "glory holes" for each arch. Some were devoted to making the lime glass used for windows and lamps; others provided the glassblowers with lead glass. There were more than 200 employees on Tiffany's payroll at the time, producing nearly 20,000 vases and bowls in a year. The simpler ones could be made at the rate of four per hour by each shop. The annealing process required one week, after which the piece was handled in the finishing department, where it was polished and registered.

Tiffany glass was marked and numbered only when it was sent out from the factory storerooms. The numbers on Tiffany vases can be an aid to dating, but only as a *terminus ante quem*. For instance, an important group of early pieces was not numbered until 1921, when it was acquired by A. Douglas Nash, the son of Arthur Nash, who became foreman after Tiffany's retirement in 1919. Other pieces taken home by employees, or those not sold before 1928, were not marked or numbered in any way. Neither were those that were dispersed during the first two years.

The registration of Tiffany glass began in 1894 with the number "A1." The Appendix includes an approximate table of the sequence of these registry numbers, for the convenience of the collector. One fairly certain conclusion to be drawn from this table is that any piece of Tiffany blown glass *authentically* marked with a number bearing a prefix letter from A to N was made no later than 1900.

The only eyewitness account of the work in Tiffany's furnaces was written by S. Bing and published in volume one of *Kunst und Kunsthandwerk* in 1898. Of course Bing was one of Tiffany's most enthusiastic admirers and his chief promoter in the European market. The account reads as follows:

Louis C. Tiffany's
COLOURED GLASS WORK[13]

Louis C. Tiffany is the son of the celebrated New York jeweller and goldsmith, Charles Tiffany, who for more than twenty years has enjoyed a world-wide reputation. Of an idealistic temperament, the young man at first devoted his youthful ardour to the study of painting. The refined feeling which that art instils into its votaries was, with him, displayed in a passionate enthusiasm for colour—rich and luminous colour. His acute sense of, and appreciation for, harmonious tints was a natural gift, but it strengthened gradually with use, and was perfected to a supreme degree during his long voyages in the East; and so Tiffany was inevitably led to exercise his creative talents in a less restricted field than painting, in a more fruitful province long unrecognised—the Decorative Arts.

What impressed the young artist and filled his heart with a transport of emotion never felt before, was the sight of the Byzantine basilicas, with their dazzling mosaics, wherein were synthesised all the essential laws and all the imaginable possibilities of the great art of decoration. Exploring the depths of a far-distant and glorious past with the aid of these venerable monuments, Tiffany dreamed a dream of Art for the Future: in the fossilised remains of our ancient patrimony were revealed

1.   Vase of opaque iridescent glass, copper red with gold overlay decoration inscribed "L. C. Tiffany–Favrile 54A–Coll." 18 cm. *Author's collection, courtesy of* The Magazine ANTIQUES
→

to him the primordial principles that live for all time. In thus evoking the souvenirs of bygone ages, the danger was that he might arrest the flow of the bold and spontaneous conceptions which are the strength of the innovator. How many partisans of a resurrection of the Decorative Arts had made shipwreck in that way! But it has been given to the youthful American race to profit by our old traditions in a more broad-minded spirit, while at the same time preserving the transatlantic love of independence. Moreover, America has always been distinguished for its capacity to bring its enterprises into perfect keeping with one another, and to direct all its energies and activity towards a definite object, in conformity with the needs of the time.

At the moment of which we speak a remarkable impetus had been given to the art of Architecture in the New World. In all directions were springing up great edifices, whose construction was, as to essential points, in accord with the cardinal principles that had come down from the early Middle Ages, while in many important respects it had been cunningly modified in an original manner rigorously adapted to the most modern requirements. Herein Tiffany saw a providential means of realising his new aesthetic visions of Decorative Art. No two arts could do better work in unison. At the same time the creators of Decorative Art were bound more than architects not to follow blindly the practice of former days. In what he did toward the beautifying of great and sumptuous habitations, our innovator was able to utilise the hieratic splendour of the orientals in a manner agreeable to contemporary tastes. He softened the boldness of Byzantine pomp into tender harmonies of

colour and effect, suitable to the decoration of the apartments in which we spend the greater part of our time. Thus the walls of a spacious hall would be a sober dead white, or finely rendered tints approximating thereto, surmounted now and then with polychrome friezes diapered with the thousand details of a cashmere design. In another place mosaic clothed the walls with warmth and sweetness, like that of silky stuffs; while on stairs, ceilings and cornices, it appeared in all its strength and brilliancy, but always preserving, both as to design and tones, an indisputably modern character. Besides being utilised in mosaic work, glass appeared in indoor decoration, in the form of windows and lighting devices; wherever, in fact, its sparkling reflections might add a joyous note to the play of light.

But before all and above all it was coloured glass that occupied the first place in Tiffany's researches. For a long time, indeed, his mind had been engrossed by the study of an important problem; namely, the discovery of a means of restoring to stained glass that purity and brilliancy the secret of which appeared to have been lost during a long series of centuries. He found that, even in the best modern specimens, the workmanship of the glass craftsman was not equal to that of the designer, each of the two collaborators being too closely mindful of his own particular task to labour in full sympathy with the other, so as to produce a homogeneous piece of work. Besides, when Tiffany considered the impressive richness of the stained glass seen in some of the Gothic cathedrals, the materials used in the present day were in comparison extremely weak, without consistency or scintillating power. Then, added to cold transparency, in which

2.   Window screen of opalescent leaded glass made in 1880 by Louis C. Tiffany for his Bella apartment in New York (see fig. 35). 60 cm., 72.5 cm. *Author's collection, courtesy of* The Magazine ANTIQUES

Window of opalescent leaded glass designed by Henri de Toulouse-Lautrec and made by the Tiffany Glass Company in 1894 (see fig. 41). 1 m. 20 m., 85 cm. *Collection of Henry Dauberville, Paris*

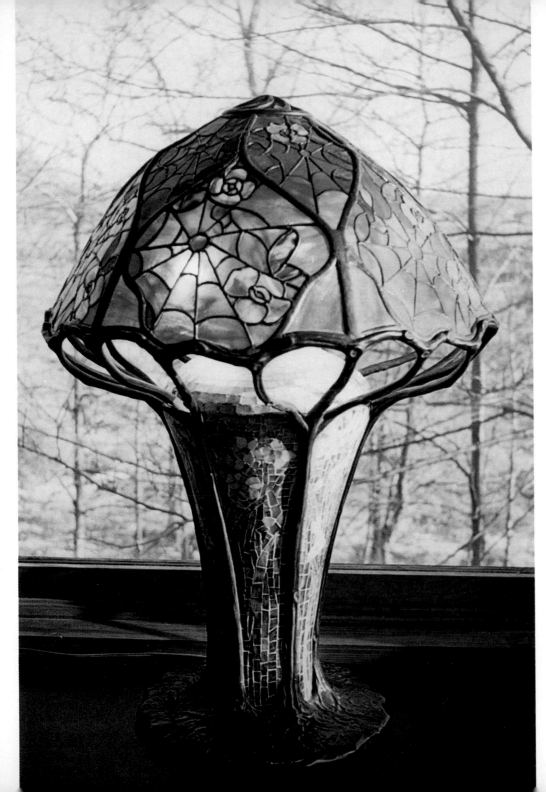

4. Bronze and coppered glass electric lamp with a glass mosaic floral design on the base and cobweb design shade inscribed "Tiffany Studios, New York 1146" circa 1902. *Private collection*

5. Unique centerpiece-lamp combination of peacock design by Tiffany
Studios of gilt bronze with iridescent glass mosaic and a coppered glass
shade, numbered "E 65." *Collection of Gladys Koch Antiques*

6–9.   Four vases purchased from the Tiffany Glass and Decorating Company,
New York, in 1897. Original Tiffany registry numbers from left to right: 4373, 318,
X2971, 1163. *Collection of the Cincinnati Museum of Art, Cincinnati, Ohio*

10.   Iridescent glass and silvered metal punch bowl made by Tiffany Studios for the Paris Exposition of 1900 (see fig. 87). 36 cm. *Collection of the Virginia Museum of Fine Arts, Richmond, Virginia*

11–13.   Varied group of Tiffany glass items in private collections.

14–17. Four photographs showing five vases, one bowl, and one plaque, all of Tiffany glass. *Collection of the Chrysler Museum, Norfolk, Virginia*

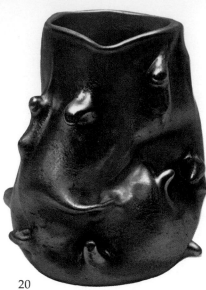

18

20

21

19

18.   Cypriote vase with fused overlay decoration inscribed "L. C. T. K1374" with original label in use prior to 1902, capped with a copper rim inscribed "Tiffany & Co." made in 1899, 25 cm. *Collection of Gladys Koch Antiques*

19.   All gold "lava" inscribed "L. C. T. 8295A" with original label in use after 1902. 12 cm. *Author's collection*

20.   Irregularly shaped vase of gold iridescent glass inscribed "L. C. Tiffany–Favrile 2184C." 11 cm. *Author's collection*

21.   Blow-out technique vase inscribed "L. C. T." 7 cm. *Private collection*

22.   "Lava" glass bowl inscribed "L. C. Tiffany–Favrile ⟶ 22 A–Coll." 14.5 cm. *Author's collection, courtesy of* The Magazine ANTIQUES

23.   Five vases from the Coats-Connelly Collection sold in 1966, courtesy of Sotheby Parke Bernet. Descriptions from the catalog (*left to right*):

1.   Green and white clear paperweight vase. Sharply tapering vase with a frieze of white lilies of the valley at the shoulder above upright yellowish-green leaves. Inscribed "L. C. T. T450." H.16.5 cm.

2.   Red and green miniature vase having slightly waisted sides and an allover pattern of green vines and stylized blossoms on an amber-red ground. Inscribed "L. C. Tiffany–Favrile, 167A–Coll." H.6.3 cm.

3.   Red vase having swelling sides and a pattern of iridescent vines bearing greenish-yellow leaf forms, a molded diamond-quilted pattern toward the base. Inscribed "L. C. Tiffany–Favrile, 114A–Coll." H.15.2 cm.

4.   Red vase urn-shaped, the lower half with large upright leaflike forms, in amber and purple iridescence. Inscribed "L. C. Tiffany–Favrile, 1722G." H.8.5 cm.

5.   Green and brown paperweight ovate vase patterned in tones of emerald green, deep green and brown with vine and rootlike shapes, the interior with silver iridescence; blown aperture at base. Inscribed "L. C. T." and "L. C. Tiffany–Favrile, Y3116." H.17.7 cm.

24.   Five vases from the Coats-Connelly Collection sold in 1966, courtesy of Sotheby Parke Bernet. Descriptions from the catalog (*counterclockwise from left*):

1.   Red paperweight vase. Ovoid vase with a frieze of elongated undersea forms interspersed with starfish. Small abrasion at shoulder. Inscribed "L. C. Tiffany–Favrile, 4A–Coll." H.13.3 cm.

2.   Red vase. Ovoid red vase decorated at the shoulder with scrolled lappets edged in sapphire blue and red on an ivory ground. Inscribed "L. C. Tiffany–Favrile, 199A–Coll." H.11.4 cm.

3.   Green and yellow agate vase. Faceted vase, the lower half marbled in tones of green, blue, and ochre. Inscribed "L. C. Tiffany–Favrile, 104A–Coll." H.8.2 cm.

4.   Green and orange paperweight vase. Slightly pyriform vessel, the lower half with a broad banding mottled in orange, brown, and green and crested with swirls; shading from milky white at the lip to amber. Inscribed "L. C. T., Y5402." H.19.6 cm.

5.   Green and blue clear paperweight vase. Baluster-shaped vase decorated at the shoulder with blue convolvulae and green leaves. Inscribed "L. C. Tiffany, 1362J." H.15.8 cm

25. Vase of Tiffany glass in the
paperweight technique, H. 19 cm.
Collection of Edgar Kaufman Jr.,
courtesy of Du

26. Vase of Tiffany peacock glass
with feather and eye decoration.
H.26.9 cm. *Collection of The Metropoli-*
tan Museum of Art, New York. Gift of the
Louis Comfort Tiffany Foundation 1951.
Courtesy of Du

27

29

30

27. Vase of carved cameo glass marked "1747C." H.29.2 cm.
Collection of the Haworth Art Gallery, Accrington, Lancashire,
England. Gift of the family of Joseph Briggs

28. Vase of aquamarine glass marked "1999H." H.10.5 cm.
Collection of the Haworth Art Gallery, Accrington, Lancashire,
England. Gift of the family of Joseph Briggs

29. Vase of Cypriote glass marked "K1354." H.27.9 cm.
Collection of the Haworth Art Gallery, Accrington, Lancashire,
England. Gift of the family of Joseph Briggs

30. Vase of faceted agate glass marked "5025E." H.19 cm.
Collection of the Haworth Art Gallery, Accrington, Lancashire,
England. Gift of the family of Joseph Briggs

28

poverty of colour alternated with a shocking hardness, there was another and still worse defect. It had long been the custom to intercept the vibrations of light by the application of pigments with a brush, thus dulling the material instead of enriching it. This was painting upon glass, not the creation of a picture from the vitreous substance itself by the juxtaposition of pieces, each one transfused with the colour appropriate to it, throughout its entire thickness.

This latter system was the one always employed up to the twelfth century, when the abuse, of painting upon glass, began to prevail. The decorative requirements of the Middle Ages were less exacting than is the case in modern times; the primitive simplicity which suited the old cathedrals scarcely sufficed for our blasé eyes, especially when the stained glass was intended to be an element of household decoration. Consequently, when something more than simple lines was needed, when it was desired to reproduce studies in the round, with strong reliefs and contrasts of light and shade, new resources had to be drawn upon and means of expression found which our ancestors had never needed. For years Tiffany gave himself up to these engrossing researches, and gradually succeeded in making a glass which answered the requirements to a wonderful degree. By the blending of colour he causes the sheet of glass to convey the effect of a cloudy sky, or of rippling water, or again the delicate shades of flowers and foliage. For drapery, in all its truth of suppleness and outline, he operates in a most ingenious manner upon the material while it is cooling, putting into it an infinite variety of folds and wrinkles. Even then he has not done perfecting, but can

communicate to the glass quite a special plastic surface. New tones are to be found on his palette, and he has quite new processes, as for instance the superposition of several plates of different colours, by which the aspect of the work is changed in the most unexpected ways.

Having thus created a material which is admirable in every respect, possessing qualities quite unknown till now, Tiffany gave it the name of "Favrile Glass," and proposed to use it for other purposes than the making of stained-glass windows. His great ambition was to employ it in the manufacture of objets d'art.

In view of the prestige of the old Venetian glassware, so elegant as to outline, but somewhat too frail and artificial; after the delicate jewellery of the Chinese glassworkers, who treated their curious material as they would the rarest cameos; after the wonderful progress realised in vitreous art in Bohemia; after the astonishing work produced by Emile Gallé; in presence of all these marvels, could inventive genius be expected to go farther?

Not for an instant did the idea occur to Tiffany to seek to excel in regard to florid ornament or patient labour; his plan was quite different from that hitherto adopted; he sought to go back to the primitive starting-point, and inaugurate a school, in which the supreme refinement of taste and learned technique should be concealed under the most modest exterior; everything should have the ease and softness and spontaneity of Nature herself. He showed us the delightfully soft effect produced by semi-opaque tints, in which were found, amalgamated with the vitreous material, fine veins and filaments, and blushes of colour similar to the delicate shades observable *in the skin of fruit, the petal of the flower, and in the "sere and yellow leaf." And in the artist's hands there grew vegetable, fruit, and flower forms, all which, while not copied from Nature in a servile manner, gave one the impression of real growth and life.*

Other examples showed a different order of motifs. *Tiffany denied that the vitreous substance should always be used exclusively as a medium for the filtration of light, on pretence that tradition had so willed it. He maintained that the artist might invest his material with another and different character, provided he did not imitate any other substance with it. Wherefore he created certain kinds of opaque and opalescent glasses, the beauty of which resided in their incomparably smooth surfaces, exquisitely soft to the touch, giving the impression of a delicate silky epidermis.*

But Tiffany had no sooner overcome one difficulty than he attacked a fresh problem. From infancy his colourist's eye had passionately loved the rich effects produced in antique glass in the course of centuries. While as yet almost a child, he had greedily sought for a few of these magic relics of the past, and his search was greatly facilitated by his father's position. Even now, on crossing the threshold of Louis Tiffany's habitation, the visitor pauses to marvel in presence of an incomparable spectacle: a large panel forming the back of the fireplace, and entirely made up of little pieces of antique glass, forms a mosaic, the like of which never was seen, whose pieces, all of irregular shape, are let into a leaden framework, similar to that of a stained-glass window.

And now that he felt he exercised mastery over the material, the idea occurred to him to create, by his art, beauties analogous to those which, up till then, had been produced very crudely, except by the fortuitous action of time. Long and patiently did he labour before securing the result of his discoveries, but at last he did attain a definite result. Far from recalling in any aspect the hard and superficial reflected lights of which certain glassworkers and ceramists seemed to be so proud, and which were only the easy product of a vulgar taste, the iridescent effects obtained by Tiffany were refined to a supreme degree. They captivated the eye by reason of their wonderful* mat *softness, and, at the same time, of a nacreous richness over which played, according to the breaking of the light, an infinite variety of tones, and wherein were opalised radiations, so subtle, delicate, and mysterious, that the water of an exquisite pearl can alone be compared to them. Herein was incarnated all the resurrected beauty of the antique glasswork, with the superadded conviction to the connoisseur that the irradiating effect was not given in this case by a change in the substance through disintegration, but that all we can see formed an integral part of the article, and was solid and firm to the touch.*

The process by which this result is obtained can be easily explained. The glass, while still hot, is exposed to the fumes produced by different metals vaporised. Evidently nothing could be simpler in principle; the secret resides in the artistic brain and cunning hand of him who performs the operation.

At the culminating-point, where the present century succeeded to the possession of the old culture, which, after climbing step by step up the ladder of Art, was hampered as to future achievements with the vast accumulation of knowledge bequeathed by our earlier ancestors, it has become difficult to propound any art principles that shall be entirely free from the prejudices of past times. The ambition of our epoch ought to be confined to the development, in a different and progressive sense, of the beautiful growths of former ages. We have seen how, in the vitreous art, Tiffany turned to good account the examples handed down from antiquity.

Every one knows what a charming effect is produced in Murano's glasswork by the innumerable ornamental lines that striate the material in all directions. They take the most picturesque forms when manipulated by the glassblower. Tiffany, owing to his superior science, more fertile imagination and better taste, was able to secure effects of which none of his predecessors had ever dreamed. He controls chance to the interpretation of his own fancy.

Look at the incandescent ball of glass as it comes out of the furnace; it is slightly dilated by an initial inspiration of air. The workman charges it at certain pre-arranged points with small quantities of glass, of different textures and different colours, and in the operation is hidden the germ of the intended ornamentation. The little ball is then returned to the fire to be heated. Again it is subjected to a similar treatment (the process being sometimes repeated as many as twenty times), and, when all the different glasses have been combined and manipulated in different ways, and the article has been brought to its definite state as to form and dimensions, it presents the following appearance: The motifs introduced into the ball when it was small have grown with the vase itself, but in differing proportions; they have lengthened or broadened out, while each tiny ornament fills the place assigned to it in advance in the mind of the artist.

For some years already Tiffany had been able to produce in this way the veining of leaves, the outlines of the petals of flowers. In the material there flowed meandering waters and fantastic cloud forms. But he was only waiting the opportunity to apply his process on a more intricate scale. Having, at the instance of an amateur friend, sought to produce in coloured glass the peacock in all the glory of his plumage, he saw in this motif a theme admirably adapted to enable him to display his skill in glass-blowing—the peacock's feather. For a whole year he pursued his studies with feverish activity, and when at last a large group of vases had been completed embodying this ideal adornment, no two of which were alike, the result was a dazzling revelation.

Just as in the natural feather itself, we find here a suggestion of the impalpable, the tenuity of the fronds and their pliability—all this intimately incorporated with the texture of the substance which serves as background for the ornament. Never, perhaps, has any man carried to greater perfection the art of faithfully rendering Nature in her most seductive aspects, while subjecting her with so much sagacity to the wholesome canons of decoration. And, on the other hand, this power which the artist possesses of assigning in advance to each morsel of glass, whatever its colour or chemical composition, the exact place which it is to occupy when the article leaves the glassblower's hands—this truly unique art is combined in these peacocks' feathers with the charm of iridescence which bathes the subtle and *velvety ornamentation with an almost supernatural light.*

If, in conclusion, we are called upon to declare the supreme characteristic of this glasswork, the essential trait that entitles it to be considered as marking an evolution in the art, we would say it resides in the fact that the means employed for the purpose of ornamentation, even the richest and most complicated, are sought and found in the vitreous substance itself, without the use of either brush, wheel, or acid. When cool, the article is finished.

S. Bing
(Translator not known)

4 ❀ VARIATIONS IN GLASS

The high point of the success of Louis C. Tiffany's career came at the Paris International Exposition in 1900. There he won a gold medal and was decorated as a Chevalier of the Legion of Honor. His exhibition punch bowl was selected as his most important contribution (Ill. 10). When, in 1970, it was again shown at the Metropolitan Museum of Art, it was characterized as "astonishing" and "in keeping with art nouveau principles."[14] It is indeed one of the most wholly Art Nouveau objects ever created in America.

But Tiffany himself was not satisfied; he had to try constantly to improve his line. On his return from Paris, he directed his glassworkers to expand the spectrum of colors. Martin Bach, the mixer, resisted this order and was forced to resign in 1902. Soon thereafter Bach established the Quezal Art Glass Company in Brooklyn, New York, where, working with Tiffany's formulas for iridescence, he produced vases and lamps from more rigid designs, more regular and more refined than those of Tiffany.

John Hollingsworth, who by 1900 had his own shop, had started at Tiffany Furnaces as Manderson's assistant and was first to respond to his employer with a spectacular shape. This was a variation of the flower-form vase known as jack-in-the-pulpit. The idea was not new, as such shapes have a long tradition in American blown glass, but as the vase was made at the Corona factory, it had a completely new look (Ill. 107). The flaring top was expanded to the limit of the material's endurance, making it a surface to display the iridescence or the decorations in the body. With the irregular undulations of the glass and a stretched edge, these vases were an amazing medium for displaying the changing color of iridescence in Favrile glass.

Next came the introduction of a wide range of new colors, the most dramatic of which was a gold ruby red. Each time a new batch of this red glass was being prepared, it had to wait until Tiffany himself arrived and personally provided the gold, in the form of twenty-dollar gold coins. That was always an event at the factory. But the new colors were not a great success on the market. Gold iridescent remained as the most popular of them. In 1901, at the Pan-American Exposition in Buffalo, New York, more than 3,000 pieces of Tiffany Favrile glass were on display, no two exactly the same in design and color. Writing in *Art de Décoration* in July 1903, the French critic M. Verneuil noted the change as follows:

The name of Tiffany promised us an admirable display, but we must confess to have been deeply disappointed. Still, we may hope that the objects exhibited do not indicate a new impulse and direction in this artistic enterprise, since, with the exception of a few pieces recalling the old Tiffany ware with all its harmonious and sumptuous

19

qualities, there is absolutely nothing to observe among these pieces, heavy yet weak in form, and with vivid yet inharmonius coloring. . . . We are indeed far from the exquisite specimens of Mr. Tiffany's earlier manner, in which the gamut of rich golds sang so superbly.[15]

But not all the critics agreed. The pages of *The Craftsman* were full of praise for the new colors and varieties of Tiffany glass, which made unlimited combinations possible. One extraordinary example of the new effects in glass introduced by Tiffany a few years later was his aquamarine glass, which was first produced in 1913.

Arthur Saunders, the glassblower, was sent by Tiffany on an all-expense-paid trip to the Bahamas with instructions to spend as much time as possible looking at underwater life from a glass-bottom boat. On his return he was given one year to do nothing else but develop the means to produce the desired effect. Only a small percentage of his experiments survived the cooling and annealing process, and the waste of time and materials was enormous. The final results, however, were unlike anything that had ever been done before. They were described in an article by Elizabeth Lounsbery, which is reprinted here in full to dispel any false notions about the nature of this type of work.

Of the many forms to which glass has been adapted, the ornamental has proved quite as necessary as the glass of utility since the earliest days of its usage, and it is in one of its most decorative and unusual forms that it is presented in the aquamarine glass, illustrated in this article, which was designed by the American artist, Louis C. Tiffany.

In imitation of the effects obtained by looking through a glass-bottomed boat, such as are used in tropical waters and from other aspects of beautifully colored water, clear and deep, this glass was conceived, in which sea vegetation, fish and seaweed are reproduced in a most realistic manner by the subtle chemistry of glass making, in which the glass is partly blown and partly left in a solid form with the objects of decoration disposed within its solid mass.

Except in the matter of shape, which is designed to conform as nearly as possible to the object of decoration that it contains, no definite design is followed by the glass blower, his idea being to produce a certain character of work, and, while he may depart from the direct scheme, the ultimate object is never lost sight of. An example of this glass often weighing twenty-five pounds is manipulated by the glass worker at the end of a five-foot blow-iron or "pontil" and takes several hours to evolve. Many pieces are lost in "annealing" the glass, in spite of the care used during the long period necessary to complete this part of the work.

Although not really belonging to this group of

aquamarine glass, though suggestive of it, is the bowl-shaped vase decorated with sprays of white blossoms and green leaves. The peculiarity of this piece is that when held in a certain position the decoration appears to be both inside and outside the bowl, although it is actually only upon the outside. This is due to the peculiarities of the "lens" principle upon which the lower part of the vase is based.

Fascinating in their naturalness are the fish subjects, in which the vase with the phantom-like schools of fish, all swimming in one direction, is particularly effective in its reproduction of their illusive qualities. The shape of the vase is made to enable the fish to be seen readily from any point. Another example shows a fish diving into an entangled net. The fish itself is absolutely transparent, and can only be seen when the vase is held in a certain light, but the vase is designed to enable one to place it in such a position that the fish will be readily visible.

In one of the vases suggesting a compote is shown a seaweed-covered rock upon which are disposed a variety of sea anemones in natural colors, the entire motif being encased in a solid mass of clear, water-like glass.

An attractive piece for the living-room table which can be used to hold tall grasses or flowers, is one of the largest vases illustrated, and represents gold fish playfully darting through masses of lacey, diaphanous seaweed. The effect is distinctly one of motion and not of solid objects imprisoned

within a mass of solid glass. Ths is designed to show a distinct water line and produces an actual one. In the subjects in which fish are used as the motif of decoration, a dragon-fly hovering over the surface of the water adds greatly to the decorative effect, as well as to the illusion.

Still another example is designed to represent a jelly fish, its translucent body apparently floating through the water. The shape is made to conform to the decoration in the base of the vase, allowing the upper part to be used for flowers if desired, as in most of these vases.

In the artistic glass-making of France to-day, and even the Venetian glass of the Renaissance, together with the various productions of the Saracens, Romans, and Egyptians, nothing so unique and illusive as these examples can be found, which is so equally adaptable to the decoration of the country as well as the city house.[16]

Besides the vases described, a few aquamarine doorstops were made, several of which Tiffany kept in his own collection. Other than these, no true paperweights have been documented that were made entirely of Tiffany glass. In relation to Tiffany, the term "paperweight" is frequently used to refer only to vases using millefiori canes encased in clear or highly transparent glass for its lens effect.

After 1900, carved cameo and carved clear crystal glass were made at Tiffany Furnaces in some cases to create the effect of rock crystal. These are listed and described in a Tiffany and Company booklet in 1911. Both cameo and intaglio carving sometimes appear on the same vase (Ill. 108).

The last of the innovations made before 1919, when Tiffany retired, was a new line of colors for table glass. These are pale pastel colors with an iridescence less dense than on the earlier golds and blues. For nearly twenty years matched sets of finger bowls, glasses, compotes, and the like had been best sellers and the most financially successful line of Tiffany glass. Gold had always outsold the blue, but now the new line of pastel colors was an immediate success. Greens, pinks, yellows, violets, whites, and combinations of these made an impressive display. When A. Douglas Nash succeeded Tiffany as the supervisor of the plant, these were featured. But Tiffany, in his retirement, was not pleased with Nash's operation of the plant, and in 1928 he withdrew his financial support. Three years later the fires of Tiffany Furnaces were extinguished and the remaining stock was dispersed in a series of sales.

It is impossible to classify all the various types of Tiffany glass produced in the more than thirty-five years of the factory's existence. The ledgers that contained the registry numbers have been lost or destroyed. The craftsmen worked on a day-to-day basis, with new instructions, new shapes, and new colors constantly being introduced either by Tiffany or by one of the members of the Nash family—with Tiffany's approval. Blackboards were used to convey these instructions to the shops and were erased when the job was done. New and unusual types of Tiffany glass appeared from time to time, and these are often difficult to describe. Some of the terms most frequently used to describe this glass are explained below:

Agate. Made by mixing various colored glasses and stirring them to obtain layers. Agate was usually opaque and was often cut, carved, or faceted to show the variations of color. It is heavier and thicker than laminated glass, which is mixed in the same way.

Aquamarine glass (described at length above). It is built like a paperweight, of light green transparent glass, with underwater scenes or fishes embedded in the interior.

Blowout glass. This has bulges blown from the inside of partly solidified glass through openings cut for the purpose, or overlay decorations to strengthen parts of the vase. No molds were ever used at Tiffany's to achieve this effect.

Cameo carved glass. Always entirely wheel-cut, never acid-etched, although acid was sometimes used to produce a matte surface on portions of the design.

Chintz glass. A form usually associated with the later Nash-inspired pastel colors. It has a fine line decoration resembling fabric.

Crystal glass. Completely transparent and frequently carved to resemble rock crystal.

Cypriote glass. Its rough surface textures resemble the decomposed surfaces of Roman glass buried for centuries.

Diatreta or *basketwork glass.* Openwork glass that resembles the famous Roman vase of that name.

Intaglio carved glass. The term used for those vases with the surface cut, never etched, to enhance the design suggested by the colors in the body of the glass. Sometimes this carving was combined with cameo cutting.

Jeweled glass. This has chunks of multicolored glass inserted and only partly fused, in order to keep their character.

Laminated glass. Prepared in a manner similar to agate glass, but then blown into more extended shapes.

Lava glass, also called *volcanic.* In shapes, this is the freest, most irregular, and most varied of all, with very rough-texture surfaces and heavy overlays.

Millefiori glass. Made entirely of cross sections of millefiori canes. These canes were also frequently inserted as a form of decoration or to produce floral effects in many other Tiffany vases.

Overlay glass. A term used to describe pieces on which the decoration appears raised from the surface because it is not entirely fused into the body of the vessel.

Paperweight-technique glass. Glass with a clear casing on the outside and an iridescent lining, highly transparent, frequently with floral effects that are better described as "underwater." There are many objections to the use of the term "paperweight," but no better designation has come forward. One collector has suggested "internal luster," and others use the term "aquamarine"; neither is adequate.[17]

Peacock glass. Readily recognizable by its similarity to the tail feathers of the bird of that name.

Reactive glass. Glass that changes its color during the process of being heated or cooled. It can be identified only by the subtle changes of tone and color on the finished product.

Many other terms have been used to describe the decorations on Tiffany glass, including the names of plants and flowers that appear to have inspired the designs. In spite of this great variety, there is an amazing consistency in style. The unifying factor is the complete absorption of High Art Nouveau that Louis C. Tiffany imparted to all the workmen under his direct supervision.

Most of the unique and important examples of the products of Tiffany's factory can be identified, and many can be dated by the marks and numbers engraved on their bases. These signatures, done by many different workers in the finishing rooms of the studios, vary greatly in size, shape, and character. One of the men was expert at making a facsimile of Tiffany's manuscript signature; others used only his initials. It is virtually impossible today to identify a modern forgery of a Tiffany mark. The glass has to be recognized by its distinctive character.

The system used for numbering the glass was revealed in a letter published in *Antiques* in 1926.[18] (See also page 40.)

5 ❦ COMMERCIAL GLASS AND OTHER PRODUCTS

In 1902, Louis C. Tiffany's father passed away and left the bulk of his estate to his artist son. This provided the creator of Tiffany glass with two new opportunities that occupied him for more than a decade.

As soon as the estate was settled, he began to design a huge mansion to perpetuate his creations and his concepts of beauty. It was to be a museum of decorative arts housing his various collections and an art school where young artists could be inspired by both the natural beauty of the setting and the objects placed in the several structures on the property. He selected a site on the north shore of Long Island near Oyster Bay, facing out on Cold Spring Harbor, and named the main house Laurelton Hall after a resort hotel that had once stood at this location. The largest of the buildings was completed in 1905, but the first group of students was not invited to reside on the premises until 1919, the year that Tiffany retired from active management of his glass factory. Organized as the Louis Comfort Tiffany Foundation, the school continued in operation, as the founder had intended, until 1942.[19]

In addition, the death of the elder Tiffany gave his son the opportunity to assume a more active role in Tiffany and Company and thereby have a new and more effective outlet for his products. Here he established new departments of Tiffany Art Jewelry, Tiffany Enamel, Tiffany Favrile Glass and Metal Ware, Tiffany Favrile Lamps, and Tiffany Favrile Pottery.

Free-blown glass hollow ware was produced and sold in great quantity for over a decade. More than a dozen different styles of bowls and glasses could be purchased as stock items in either gold or blue luster, with or without engraved leaf and vine decoration. The gold was the most popular and is still the more available, although today the blue is considered the more desirable. Pattern names include Ascot, Colonial, Dominion, Earl (stretched edge), Flemish (threaded), Iris (decorated in the glass), Manhattan, Prince, Queen (fluted edge), Royal (twisted stem), Savoy, and Victoria.[20] After 1900, these were not registered with the same numbering system used for unique vases. Many of them that bear the Tiffany name or initials have no numbers, whereas others were numbered sequentially with numbers but no letter of the alphabet. This also applies to many of the blown-glass shades of various shapes and sizes that were made for a variety of lighting fixtures.

Recognition and identification of the hollow ware made by Tiffany glassworkers are often difficult, as it was imitated in both Europe and America, in some cases by glassmen formerly employed at the Corona plant. To complicate the matter still further, forged marks have begun to appear on glass that was made by others. Nevertheless, all Tiffany glass has a distinctive quality

25

that can be recognized by a connoisseur who has sufficient experience with well-documented examples.

At the Louisiana Purchase Exposition in St. Louis, Missouri, in 1904, Tiffany introduced several new products under the auspices of Tiffany Studios in collaboration with Tiffany and Company, including jewelry, enamels, and pottery. There were 25 pieces of jewelry designed by Louis C. Tiffany, made and lent by Tiffany and Company[21]—ornaments, tiaras, pins, a girdle, and a necklace of gold and silver set with gemstones and enameled. These were simply marked "Tiffany and Company," and so there is no way to distinguish them from the regular line of the firm except on the basis of style. Their Art Nouveau forms, their inspiration from nature, and their combinations of color are unmistakable. The same principles that governed the designs of windows, glass, and lamps apply to the jewelry.

Also in St. Louis in 1904—lent by Tiffany Furnaces and designed by Louis C. Tiffany—were 40 pieces of Favrile glass, 12 copper vases and bowls "enriched with translucent enamels," and three pieces of Favrile pottery.[22] After 1904, these new products were produced in quantity according to their sales. The line of jewelry was expanded to include belts, bracelets, brooches, charms, cuff links, earrings, hatpins, rings, and even stoles, the latter "of coral beads with pierced gold ornaments set with amethysts."[23]

Tiffany and Company also made and sold a line of "Favrile Beetle Jewelry" consisting of belts, belt pins, charms, hatpins, necklaces, pendants, scarf pins, studs, and watch guards of Favrile glass scarabs set in 18-karat gold. The scarab beetle Favrile glass jewels were pressed at Tiffany's glass furnaces and mounted at Tiffany and Company. The jewels are not marked, and the gold is stamped with only the company name.

Glass presses were used only for jewels and tiles. The rule that all Tiffany hollow ware must be free blown was almost never violated. The use of molds was also prohibited, in the interest of variety and preserving the true meaning of Favrile. The handmade quality of Tiffany glass justifies the claim that every piece is unique. Even in matched sets there are differences of size and color qualities that are often obvious. The workmen were never urged to stress regularity and refinement. The result is the most apparent characteristic of Tiffany glass, the one that distinguishes it from its closest competitors: uniqueness.

In spite of the declining popularity of Art Nouveau in elite circles, the production of Tiffany glass and other products continued at full speed until the First World War. The Tiffany name was a status symbol, a guarantee of the finest quality, and a Tiffany product was deemed an ideal gift item for any occasion. New patterns continued to be introduced and exhibited in the various show-rooms, and elaborate examples were made to be sent to exhibitions wherever possible. Tiffany and Company had outlets in London and Paris that served as foreign distributors of the glass and metal objects after the death of S. Bing in 1905.

Because of the war, production was curtailed in 1916 and the showrooms moved to smaller quar-ters. After the war, Louis C. Tiffany turned the business over to those managers he had carefully trained and devoted his energy to students at his Foundation on Long Island. From then on, both the quality and the designs of Tiffany products deteriorated steadily until 1928, when the factory was shut down.

6 ❧ COLLECTORS AND COLLECTIONS

Louis C. Tiffany was an avid collector, and most of the objects produced under his direct supervision were intended to be collector's items. As a youth, Tiffany had learned of the pleasures and advantages of collecting fine objects from his father's partner, the silversmith Edward C. Moore, whose collection of Oriental decorative arts has served as a nucleus of that department in the Metropolitan Museum of Art. Tiffany began with Japanese arms and armor; his closest friend and associate, the painter Samuel Colman, collected Chinese ceramics. As a decorator in the 1880s, Tiffany had many opportunities to advise his clients and to encourage them to collect. It was no accident that he and Colman decorated the Havemeyer house in 1890, and in turn the Havemeyers became the first important collectors of Tiffany's glass.

The Havemeyer gift of Tiffany glass to the Metropolitan Museum of Art in 1896 remains one of the most important examples of Tiffany's first four years' work with blown glass, rivaled only by the items acquired the same year by the Smithsonian Institution in Washington, D.C. Other American museums, including the Cincinnati Museum of Art in 1897, purchased representative pieces directly from the Tiffany Glass and Decorating Company.

In Paris the dealer S. Bing, who had been advisor to such important collectors of Japanese art as the brothers De Goncourt, became the first major collector of Tiffany glass on the Continent. He was also Tiffany's distributor for all of Europe; he organized exhibitions in London and Paris and sold Tiffany products to both collectors and museums. Tiffany glass was always featured at Bing's *Salon de l'Art Nouveau*, which opened to the public in December 1895.

Tiffany's own collection, as displayed in Laurelton Hall on Long Island after 1905, was certainly the most select. It consisted of about five hundred items selected by the artist, most of which were inscribed "A-Coll" with a number. This collection was sold at auction in 1946 along with the entire contents of Laurelton Hall, which included many Japanese tsuba, American Indian baskets, Oriental rugs and furniture, Roman glass, and miscellaneous objects too numerous to list. The sale took five days and brought over $100,000, but the Tiffany Favrile glass items did not do well—372 of these went for a total of less than $10,000. The most expensive single piece was a leaded glass ceiling light six feet in diameter—it sold for $275.[24]

Other members of the Tiffany organization also collected the glass that they were involved in producing. The collections belonging to the two sons of Arthur Nash have been disbursed without being recorded. A significant portion of the collection of English-born Joseph Briggs is known to be still intact, even though it has not yet been published. Briggs, who was responsible for carrying on the work of Tiffany Studios after the death of Louis C. Tiffany in 1933, visited the place of his birth, Accrington, Lancashire, in September 1932 and brought with him more than one hundred examples of the work of his employer; sixty-seven of these were vases of Favrile glass, the remainder were mosaics and tiles. Believed to be the largest public collection of Tiffany glass in Europe, it was donated by the Briggs family in 1933 to the Haworth Art Gallery, Accrington, where it is presently housed. If there were any other equally important contemporary collections of Tiffany products in Europe, they have not yet come to light.

During the two decades that saw the Great Depression and the Second World War, Tiffany glass was in disrepute. The Bauhaus-initiated International Style dominated the world of art, and colorful decorative arts were rejected. Then in the mid-1950s a new generation nourished a revival of interest in Art Nouveau. When an exhibition of Tiffany's work was organized in 1958, the collector contributors were George S. Barrows, Joseph Heil, Edgar Kaufmann, Jr., Hugh F. McKean, and Ward Mount.[25] The Joseph Heil Collection has since been donated to the Museum of Modern Art in New York. The McKean Collection, presently housed in Winter Park, Florida, includes the largest and most important collection of Tiffany windows in the world. McKean was first exposed

to Tiffany's work as a fellow at the Foundation in Oyster Bay, and, after the fire of 1957, he acquired whatever was salvageable from Laurelton Hall.

The New York exhibition of 1958 stimulated several new collectors, most of whom concentrated on decorated free-form vases. One of these collections, assembled by James Coats and Brian Connelly, was disbursed at auction in 1966. In that sale 76 vases brought over $85,000.[26] However, although the value of Tiffany vases had increased one hundred times in two decades, other Tiffany products had not kept pace. Only leaded glass lamps in floral designs were then being collected with the same enthusiasm that elevated the value of the vases. Walter P. Chrysler, Jr., was the first to collect lamps in a serious way. These are now in the Chrysler Museum at Norfolk, Virginia. Since 1966, the rate of increase in value of the lamps has exceeded that of the vases.

The recent discovery and reprinting of Tiffany Studios original catalogs and price lists, many of which are included in *Louis C. Tiffany's Glass—Bronzes—Lamps*, have now made it more convenient to collect metal products, such as candlesticks and desk set items, because the collector can easily check the pattern names by their model numbers. Recent sales have shown this category to be of growing interest.

The question is often asked whether these values will remain as high as they are today. The answer depends entirely on the continuing or increasing demand by collectors. The market remains free, worldwide, and without manipulation, but the supply is diminishing as donations are made to public institutions like the gift by J. Jonathan Joseph to the Museum of Fine Arts in Boston, Massachusetts, or the gift by Helmut Hentrich to the Kunstmuseum in Dusseldorf. These more than offset the new items that keep coming up on the market. As long as collectors maintain their interest, however—and none appear to be less enthusiastic at the moment—the market will remain strong. It is never too late to start collecting as long as there is the expectation that others will do likewise.

CONCLUSION

Tiffany glass is difficult to classify. Made between 1892 and 1928, it is neither ancient nor contemporary. Art Nouveau belongs to a previous era and can be called antique, yet it is clearly the first stage in the development of modern art. Its parallel in painting is the work of the Nabis and the Symbolists of the 1890s. In the history of glass it is the most daring, innovative, and creative, representing the rejection of classicism and historic conventions.

Robert Schmutzler, writing in 1962, commented:

Tiffany's formal inventiveness of form is particularly striking: in spite of the regular, uninterrupted flow of the contours and of an ornamentation solely due to the haphazard flow of molten glass, these magnificent individual pieces suggest something bizarre and extravagant which is always convincing and of great taste and distinction. . . . By means of his personal creations, however, and most of all through the glassware he produced between 1893 and 1900 that was responsible for his universal fame, . . . Tiffany became one of the most prominent artists of Art Nouveau.[27]

According to Mario Amaya in 1967:

Tiffany glass, with its swirling patterns, its strange iridescent colors, its marbled designs, its curious free-form shapes, its clear, brilliant patternings trapped as if by magic in the texture of the object, was without a doubt the most beautiful glass produced in its time.[28]

Where Tiffany succeeded was in opening up avenues of aesthetic invention to his countrymen which were not based on previous European-inspired models, but rather on nature's organic forms which owed their invention to nothing but themselves. It is this non-objective, abstract quality which perhaps helped the generation of the early 1950's to see the intrinsic merit in both Tiffany glass and Art Nouveau as it related to the avant-garde painting of the time. In fact, Favrile glass appeared as an uncanny precedent to Abstract Expressionism and when America's first great international contribution to contemporary painting was hardening into a movement in the early fifties, Tiffany glass—which itself depended so much on the principles of controlled accident, color, shape, and free-form design—found new admirers.[29]

As an abstract art form, many examples of Tiffany glass transcend the usual concept of Art Nouveau as an essentially decorative style. Expressionism is as evident in Tiffany's style as in that of Van Gogh or of Munch. Suggestions of the biomorphic and the phallic appear frequently in the forms and decorations and account for much of the negative criticism on the part of those who prefer purity in art. It is this element that sets Tiffany's product apart from those of Gallé and Lalique and accounts for his greater influence on

German and Bohemian glass designers at the turn of the century.[30]

During his lifetime, Louis C. Tiffany placed the greatest importance on his windows, as was indicated in two speeches made late in his career, in 1916 and 1917 (republished hereafter). In these he stressed the importance of color and its impact on the emotions of the observer. He is reputed to have stated that his lamps were a by-product of his windows. He saw form as merely a vehicle to carry color and movement. His art was purely instinctive and irrational. His wish to return to basics makes his creed akin to those of Kandinsky and Klee.

The painters, however, carried their concepts a step farther by including the idea of spontaneity. To this Tiffany objected; he spoke out against it as "ignoring technique."

Louis C. Tiffany was indeed one of the foremost pioneers of modern art. He made no distinction between fine and applied or decorative arts, and in his quest of beauty he advanced farther into modernism than almost any other artist of his generation. From this point of view, the abstract free-form vases created under his direct supervision were his most significant achievement.

SELECTED STATEMENTS
BY LOUIS C. TIFFANY

I. "The Quest of Beauty," presented on the occasion of the celebration of his sixty-eighth birthday in 1916.

What is the Quest of Beauty? What else is the goal that an artist sets before him, but that same spirit of beauty! Who can give the formula for it? Are there not as many different paths to it as there are workmen, and are there not as many different definitions of beauty, as there are artists? And yet I wish to express what I have found in art. How can I say briefly what I have been striving to express in art during my life?

Literature and the Drama express the sensations of tragedy and romance—but not with continuity and lasting effect. Art interprets the beauty of ideas and of visible things, making them concrete and lasting. When the savage searches for the gems from the earth or the pearls from the sea to decorate his person, or when he decorates the utensils of war or peace in designs and colours, he becomes an artist in embryo, for he has turned his face to the quest of beauty.

Art starts from an instinct in all—stronger in one than in another—and that instinct leads to the fixing of beauty in one of a hundred ways. But, if we look closer, we find some artists are drawn aside from the pursuit of beauty to worship the idol of technique, though only a small part of the effectiveness of a work of art can be credited to technique. The thirteenth century makers of stained glass were great because they saw and repro-duced beauty from the skies and stars—the gems and rugs; they translated the beauty into the speech of stained glass. In later days, ignoring the beauty of the glass by using paint, their successors destroyed by this technique the beauty for which they were striving.

If I may be forgiven a word about my own work, I would merely say that I have always striven to fix beauty in wood or stone or glass or pottery, in oil or water colour, by using whatever seemed fittest for the expression of beauty; that has been my creed, and I see no reason to change it. It seems as if the artists who place all their energies on technique have nothing left over for the more important matter—the pursuit of beauty. The 'Modernists,' as they are called for want of a better term, wander after curiosities of technique, vaguely hoping they may light on some invention which will make them famous. They do not belong to art; they are untrained inventors of processes of the arts.

One thing more—it seems to me that the majority of critics miss the chance of doing good by failing to understand the situation; too many of them waste their time in disapproval of what they dislike, instead of looking for what they can honestly admire. The public thinks that a critic is a person who attacks and condemns; a critic should be one who discriminates. The critic who can do good is one who does not neglect the high lights for the shadows, but strives to find the best points in each work of art.

II. "Color and Its Kinship to Sound," a speech before the Rembrandt Club of Brooklyn, New York, in 1917.

At present the main body of my work deals with a very brittle matter, namely glass; but the fragility of glass does not interfere with a great capacity for beauty on its part. I do not think that we often remember that glass as a vehicle for beauty has a past quite as venerable as that of other mediums, if not in the form of windows, yet in that of useful and decorative objects. And when glass was first used about the Mediterranean it was accompanied by color.

When first I had a chance to travel in the East and to paint where the people and the buildings also are clad in beautiful hues, the preeminence of color in the world was brought forcibly to my attention. I returned to New York wondering why we made so little use of our eyes, why we refrained so obstinately from taking advantage of color in our architecture and our clothing when Nature indicates its mastership, when, by its use under the rules of taste, we can extend our innocent pleasure and have more happiness in life, at the same time adding to the happiness of our neighbor.

This reluctance to enjoy what is natural and beneficent, which is found among most of the northern Europeans and Americans, makes it hard to introduce any warmth among us . . . but let me return to my own cause.

When I got back to work at home and wanted to decorate my studio and home, I was confronted amongst other problems with the question: What was to be done for the windows? since all windows were poor in quality and color! I then perceived that the glass used for claret bottles and preserve jars was richer, finer, had a more beautiful quality in color-vibrations than any glass I could buy.

So I set to puzzling out this curious matter and found that the glass from which the bottles are made contains the Oxides of Iron and other impurities which are left in the sand when that is melted. Now to extract it is costly; and so the glass-man left them there, without in the least realizing that his neglect made for beauty—and the substances he did not purge out were the very cause of that richness in the glass that I found beautiful! Refining the pot metal only made weak, uninteresting glass!

Here I met, however, the prejudice and mental habits of glassmakers. So I took up chemistry, built furnaces— two of them were destroyed by fire—and for some time my experiments met with no success. But little by little I made some steps that encouraged me. Year by year the experiments that baffled hope gave way to better results and so in the course of time through hard work and with the assistance of others, I have reached the point where it is possible to produce any color and any lustre that may be required.

Naturally I was attracted to the old glass in windows of the twelfth and thirteenth centuries which have always seemed to me the finest ever! Their rich tones are due in part to the use of pot-metal full of impurities, and in part to the uneven thickness of the glass, but still more because the glassmakers of that day abstained from the use of paint.

They had the few colors they needed in the glass itself, and that was enough.

Later the temptation to help out with paint was the beginning of deterioration in glass windows from the standpoint of art. It was necessary to struggle against this habit of makers of glass windows, which is still practised in Europe. By the aid of studies in chemistry and through years of experiments, I have found means to avoid the use of surface-painting of glass, so that now it is possible to produce figures in glass of which even the flesh tones are not superficially treated.

In Christ Church in your Borough you should examine the big window to see the proof of my statement; the heads therein are built up of what I call "genuine" glass, genuine because there are no tricks of the glassmaker needed to express the flesh.

Many of you who have not turned any particular attention to the secrets of glassmaking may be surprized at the emphasis I give to this point, but those who have had the time to look into such matters, will understand the importance of the step taken. At Laurelton Hall near Oyster Bay, I have a nude figure in glass which has no surface paint or etched parts to express the flesh, while the garments of other figures in the same composition are rendered by the artful adjustment of glass in different thicknesses. Some day I hope to have the pleasure of welcoming this worshipful company at Laurelton—it is only about twenty-five miles from here—when you can satisfy yourselves that I am not indulging in exaggeration. This is one of the most important advances in modern colored windows.

"Nature is always right"—that is a saying we often hear from the past; and here is another: "Nature is always beautiful" . . . but when someone dares to say that on the contrary "Nature is rarely right—and to such an extent even that it almost might be said that Nature is usually wrong," then the people who love Nature and are striving to follow her lead become disgusted and more than angry.

We read a great deal, and we hear it supported in the present, to the effect that all that is in Nature, all that we see and feel, is expressed to our senses by form or by lines. These discriminators between color and line put color in the background to play the second fiddle. They stoutly maintain that it is false doctrine to say that color is superior to line, a doctrine set up and defended by certain men of the early nineteenth century who are called the Romantics. Nay, some go so far as to say that the doctrine of the superiority of color to form is one concerning which you have to laugh—in order not to weep!

That is a very bad situation, is it not? But allow me to suggest an alternative, namely, to neither laugh nor weep, but just bravely consider the claims of the triumphant and cocksure Formists and the timid suggestions put forward by a humble believer in Color.

It is curious, is it not, that line and form disappear at a short distance, while color remains visible at a much longer? It is fairly certain—isn't it?—that the eyes of children at first see only colored surfaces—the breast and face of the mother, the head of the father, a colored ball or apple, the nodding crest of Hektor in Troy! Color and movement, not form, are our earliest impressions when babies. Insects are attracted by color (not form) when in search of food. For that very reason flowers develop color, because they must have the visits of insects to reproduce their kind. And if the plant has flowers that require a visit from a moth or night-flying beetle, why, then it produces—not a pink or blue blossom, which would not "carry" in the dark, but white or pale-yellow petals that call the favoring insect out of the night sky.

The Orientals have been teaching the Occidentals how to use colors for the past 10,000 years or so. Their textiles especially have been important parts of the commerce they drove with the fierce barbarians, who muttered and murmured and stuttered and jabbered incomprehensible tongues on a hundred seacoasts. In fact, barbar is only one of many words invented to imitate the sound of a language unknown to those who traded into foreign parts. The men of the East who supplied barbarians with rugs and figured textiles considered color first, and form only incidentally. Their designs were spots or tracts of color, and during the course of time they learned through reasoning and instinct that a fine design can be spoilt if the wrong combinations and juxtaposition of colors are chosen. We have to discover as they did what marvelous power one color has over another, and what the relative size of each different tract of color means to the result—what the mass of each different color means for the effect of the design as a whole!

Take a textile of Oriental make or a wall-hanging: it is fine according as the color-masses or spots are well selected and properly placed in relation one to the other. Take, on the other hand, a European textile or wall-paper where shaded flowers are introduced to enhance the design—and what a hideous result do we get for that rug or textile or wall-hanging!

Now apply the same argument to stained glass! Take a glass window of the Thirteenth Century—do we not see at once that Color is of the first importance there? With regard to the painting of flowers—there again Color is of the first importance. In many flowers their form is

distinctly a secondary consideration, which comes after the satisfaction we feel in their colors—those hues that glow and flicker and strike the sight like the embers, the little many-colored jets and the steadier flames of a drift-wood fire.

Let us take colors as the component parts in decoration. We must have a combination of the physical and mental in a fine decoration—the objective and the subjective must be married and intimately blended by the subtle employment of color, as the composer employs the moods of music.

The sovereign importance of Color is only beginning to be realized in modern times. Some people, unfortunate people, are really color-blind without their knowing it. Many more are deficient in the sense of color—and know it not. Only a few have combined with an inborn color-sense the chance to study and develop this original gift, which is given to many persons in their cradles, but is neglected afterward and even educated out of them. During childhood form is the second thing seen and form is soon made so important that color dwindles and its charm is forgot in the rush and struggle of new impressions, new ideas. It seems to me that education should strive to keep alive this primal natural instinct and never allow human beings to forget or neglect what will always prove in after-life a source of pure enjoyment such as we may imagine to be one of the delights of those beings of another world—who mayhap shall surpass the measure of human kind!

Light is composed of vibrations of differing wave-lengths, each vibration giving a different color; when all vibrate together, the result is white light. Were it not for these vibrations, what form, what lines could be seen? We could then only feel form, detect shape by the tactile sense. Let us consider now, whether those reasoners are correct who allot a secondary place to Color.

Today we are beginning to realize that these light-vibrations have a subjective power and affect the mind and soul, producing feelings and ideas of their own in the recipient brain. Light and sound are being studied in correlation, so that those who have developed the color-sense to a high degree can experience a correspondingly delicate perception in the realm of sound; and vice-versa, those who are delicately versed in sound can experience the finer impressions of the sense of sight. Instruments are being invented to prove by demonstration the subtle connection that exists between the two senses of color and sound.

Thus, photography is the image produced on sensitive surfaces by white light. Now, separate this white light into component colors, and we have color-photography.

And now to close: We are all at work toward the same ideal, which is—Beauty. That same Beauty is what Nature has lavished upon us as a Supreme Gift—it is all about us to see and use. Copying what others have done helps us indeed to exercise our eyes; but merely to copy and not to employ our imagination—is to strangle our talent, our heritage! Styles are merely the copying of what others have done, perhaps done better than we. God has given us our talents, not to copy the talents of others, but rather to use our brains and imagination in order to obtain the revelation of True Beauty!

REGISTRY NUMBERS BY YEARS

1892–93	1–9999	1911	Suffix F
1894	Prefix A and B	1912	Suffix G
1895	Prefix C and D	1913	Suffix H
1896	Prefix E and F	1914	Suffix I
1897	Prefix G and H	1915	Suffix J*
1898	Prefix I and J*	1916	Suffix K
1899	Prefix K and L	1917	Suffix L
1900	Prefix M and N*	1918	Suffix M*
1901	Prefix O and P	1919	Suffix N
1902	Prefix Q and R	1920	Suffix O
1903	Prefix S and T	1921	Suffix P
1904	Prefix U and V*	1922	Suffix Q
1905	Prefix W and Y	1923	Suffix R
1906	Suffix A*	1924	Suffix S
1907	Suffix B	1925	Suffix T
1908	Suffix C	1926	Suffix U
1909	Suffix D	1927	Suffix V
1910	Suffix E	1928	Suffix W

*Dates confirmed by exhibition pieces.

Exceptions:

Prefix "S" also used for Blown Glass Shades and Globes

Prefix "X" means "Experimental"

Prefix "EX" means "For Exhibition"

Prefix small "o" means "Special Order" (the only number system to run over 10,000)

Suffix "A-COLL" means "For Louis C. Tiffany's Private Collection" (fewer than 250 so marked)

Prefix "P" designates "Pottery"; "BP" is for "Bronze Pottery"

Prefixes "EL," "EC," "SG" designate "Enamels"

SELECT BIBLIOGRAPHY

Amaya, Mario. *Tiffany Glass*. New York: Walker & Co., 1967.

Bing, S. "Die Kunstgläser von Louis C. Tiffany." *Kunst und Kunsthandwerk*, vol. 1, 1898.

Bing, Samuel. *Artistic America, Tiffany Glass and Art Nouveau*. Cambridge, Massachusetts: The M.I.T. Press, 1970.

Bott, Gerhard. *Kunsthandwerk Um 1900* (catalog). Hessisches Landesmuseum, Darmstadt, 1965.

Cianetti, F. "Art Nouveau in New York." *DU*, no. 364, June 1971.

Clark, Robert Judson. *The Arts and Crafts Movement in America 1876–1916* (catalog). Princeton, New Jersey, 1972.

DeKay, Charles. *The Art Work of Louis C. Tiffany*. New York: Doubleday Page, 1914.

Feld, Stuart P. "Nature in Her Most Seductive Aspects." *Bulletin of the Metropolitan Museum of Art*. New York, November 1962.

Grover, Ray and Lee. *Art Glass Nouveau*. Rutland, Vermont: Charles E. Tuttle, 1967.

Hilschenz, Helga. *Glassammlung Hentrich* (catalog). Kunstmuseum, Düsseldorf, 1973.

Koch, Robert. *Louis Comfort Tiffany* (catalog). The Museum of Contemporary Crafts, New York, 1958.

———. *Louis C. Tiffany, Rebel in Glass*. New York: Crown Publishers, 1964. Second edition, New York, 1966.

———. "Tiffany Glass." *Art at Auction* 1966–67. New York: Sotheby and Company, 1967.

———. *Louis C. Tiffany's Glass—Bronzes—Lamps*. New York: Crown Publishers, 1971.

———. "Tiffany Abstractions in Glass." *Antiques*, vol. 105, no. 6, June 1974.

Madson, S. Tschudi. *Art Nouveau*. New York: McGraw-Hill, Inc., 1967.

McKean, Hugh F. *Revolt in the Parlor*. Winter Park, Florida, 1969.

Neustadt, Egon. *The Lamps of Tiffany*. New York: Fairfield Press, 1970.

Nichols, Hobart. *Favrile Glass and Enamel* (catalog). Parke-Bernet Galleries Sale number 785. New York, September 1946.

Purtell, Joseph. *The Tiffany Touch*. New York: Random House, 1971.

Revi, Albert Christian. *American Art Nouveau Glass*. New York: Thomas Nelson, 1968.

Rheims, Maurice. *L'Art 1900*. Paris: Art et Métiers Graphiques, 1965.

Schaefer, Herwin. "Tiffany's Fame in Europe." *The Art Bulletin*, vol. 44, no. 4, December 1962.

Schöenberger, Arno. *Werke Um 1900* (catalog). Kunstgewerbe Museum, Berlin, 1966.

Schmutzler, Robert. *Art Nouveau*. New York: Harry N. Abrams, Inc., 1962.

Tiffany Glass and Decorating Company. *Tiffany Favrile Glass*. New York, 1896.

Tiffany, Louis C. "American Art Supreme in Colored Glass." *The Forum,* vol. 15, 1893.

———."The Gospel of Good Taste." *Country Life In America,* vol. 29, no. 2, November 1910.

———."The Tasteful Use of Light and Color in Artificial Illumination." *Scientific American,* vol. 104, 1911.

———."What is the Quest of Beauty?" *The International Studio,* vol. 58, 1916.

———."Color and Its Kinship to Sound." *The Art World,* vol. 2, 1917.

———."The Quest of Beauty." *Harper's Bazaar,* December 1917.

Tracy, Berry B. *19th Century America, Decorative Arts* (catalog). The Metropolitan Museum of Art, New York, 1970.

Vedder, Elihu, *The Digressions of V.* Boston: Houghton Mifflin Co., 1910.

Wichmann, Siegfried. *Internationales Jugendstilglass* (catalog). Museum Stuck-Villa, Munich, 1969.

NOTES

1. Tiffany's sketchbook made during his travels in 1865–66 has recently turned up and is now in the Hugh F. McKean Collection in Winter Park, Florida. For more details of Tiffany's family and his early training, see Robert Koch, *Louis C. Tiffany, Rebel in Glass* (New York: Crown Publishers, Inc., 1964).

2. The two panels for the dining room of the Kemp house are now also in the McKean Collection. One, the gourd design, is illustrated in *The Arts and Crafts Movement in America 1876–1916*, Robert Judson Clark (editor) (Princeton, New Jersey: Princeton University Press, 1972), p. 19, figure 6.

3. Also see Robert Koch, "Tiffany Abstractions in Glass," *The Magazine Antiques*, vol. 105, no. 6 (June 1974), pp. 1288–94.

4. John LaFarge and Tiffany studied glassmaking under the same master, but became rivals after 1880 when competing to get commissions from Stanford White.

5. Bing, a native of Hamburg, had the given name of "Sigfried," but while in Paris often used the name "Samuel." His admiration for America in general and Tiffany in particular is expressed in *La Culture Artistique en Amérique*, Paris, 1895, now available in English as *Artistic America, Tiffany Glass and Art Nouveau* (Cambridge, Massachusetts: The M.I.T. Press, 1970).

6. The windows designed by Bonnard and Toulouse-Lautrec are still in existence, presently in a private collection in Paris.

7. A list compiled by Tiffany Studios in 1910 and published soon thereafter, *A Partial List of Windows*, is preserved in the Boston Public Library and has recently been republished.

8. *New York Morning Journal*, April 6, 1885.

9. The complete Tiffany Studios price list of October 1, 1906, has been republished as Appendix 1, Robert Koch, *Louis C. Tiffany's Glass—Bronzes—Lamps* (New York: Crown Publishers, Inc., 1971).

10. S. Bing, *Artistic America*, p. 146.

11. The facts given here were obtained from the late James A. Stewart, who was employed as a glassblower at Tiffany's from 1895 until 1928.

12. "An Interview with Jimmy Stewart" Robert Koch, *Louis C. Tiffany's Glass—Bronzes—Lamps*, p. 64.

13. This article was published in German as "Die kunstglaser von Louis C. Tiffany" in *Kunst und Kunsthandwerk*, vol. 1, 1898, pp. 105–11. An English translation of the article served as the introduction to the catalog of an exhibition of Tiffany products at the Grafton Galleries in London in 1899. In this form it was reprinted in S. Bing, *Artistic America*, pp. 195–212.

14. Berry B. Tracy, editor, *19th-Century America, Furniture and Other Decorative Arts* (New York: The Metropolitan Museum of Art, 1970, number 271).

15. Translated by Irene Sargent in "A Minor French Salon," *The Craftsman*, vol. 4 (1903), pp. 451–52.

16. Elizabeth Lounsbery, "Aquamarine Glass," *American Homes and Gardens*, December 1913, p. 419.

17. Albert Christian Revi, in *American Art Nouveau Glass* (New York: Thomas Nelson, 1968), p. 42, claims "Collectors and dealers refer to some internally lustred objects as 'paperweight Tiffany.' This is a manufactured nomenclature, and we sincerely hope this misnomer will be dropped from the vocabulary of Tiffany-glass terms."

18. "Questions and Answers," *Antiques*, December 1926, p. 478.

19. The mainhouse was destroyed by fire in 1957. A profusely illustrated study of the building and its contents is included in *Louis C. Tiffany: Rebel in Glass*.

20. Lists of these items appear in the Tiffany and Company *Blue Book* catalogs from 1902 until 1916.

21. These are listed in the *Official Catalogue of Exhibits, Department of Art*, St. Louis, 1904, pp. 83 and 84. This collection was then shown in Paris at the Salon of 1905 and published in *The International Studio*, December 1906, pages XXXII to XLII. One of these items, the Peacock Necklace, is in the collection of Hugh F. McKean.

22. Martin P. Eidelberg, "Tiffany Favrile Pottery," *The Connoisseur*, September 1968, pp. 57–61.

23. Tiffany and Company, *Blue Book of 1911*, p. 612.

24. Catalog 785, *Objects of Art*, Parke-Bernet Galleries, Inc., New York, September 24–28, 1946.

25. *Louis Comfort Tiffany* (catalog), Museum of Contemporary Crafts, New York, 1958. Two prominent dealers, Maude B. Feld and Lillian Nassau, also contributed to this exhibition.

26. Sale Number 2465, *Tiffany Glass, The Coats-Connelly Collection*, Parke-Bernet Galleries, Inc., New York, October 1966.

27. Robert Schmutzler, *Art Nouveau* (New York: Harry N. Abrams, Inc., 1962), p. 230.

28. Mario Amaya, *Tiffany Glass*, Collectors Blue Books (New York: Walker and Company, 1967), p. 7.

29. Idem, pp. 82, 83.

30. The Loetz Witwe factory in Klostermühle was the first, in 1897, to produce a Tiffany-type iridescent glass. Soon thereafter the firm of Bakalowits Söhne in Vienna produced the same type glass.

PHOTO CREDITS

Ader Picard Tajan, Paris, 3

Wayne Andrews, Detroit, 36

David Aronow, New York, 114, 115, 128

George Barrows, New York, 99, 100, 101, 102

Carnegie Institute, Pittsburgh, 97

Franco Cianetti, Clohars-Carnoet, 25, 26

Cincinnati Museum of Art, Cincinnati, 6, 7, 8, 9

Molly Malone Cook, Provincetown, 59

E. de Cusati, New Haven, 107, 108, 119

Helga Studios, New York, 1, 2, 22

Hessisches Landesmuseum, Darmstadt, 44, 81, 82, 83

Walter Klein, Düsseldorf, 121, 122, 123

Robert Koch, Norwalk, 4, 5, 10, 14–17, 18–21, 90, 91, 92

Kunstgewerbemuseum, Berlin, 88, 89

George Love, Sao Paolo, 11, 12, 13, 55

Metropolitan Museum of Art, New York, 45, 53, 62–67, 118, 124–127

Musée des Arts Décoratifs, Paris, 59, 60, 61

Museum of Fine Arts, Boston, 94, 95

Museum für Kunst und Gewerbe, Hamburg, 84, 85, 86

Museum of Modern Art, New York, 98–106

North Western Museum and Art Gallery Service, Accrington, Lancashire, England, 27, 28, 29, 30

Smithsonian Institution, Washington D.C., 68–80

Sotheby Parke Bernet, New York, 23, 24

James Stewart, New York, 56, 57, 58, 116, 120

J. Szaszfai, New Haven, 34

I. de Szepessy, Paris, 43, 87

Tiffany Studios, New York, 47–51

University of Michigan, Ann Arbor, 46

Victoria and Albert Museum, London, 54, 107–13

Walters Art Gallery, Baltimore, 96

A. J. Wyatt, Philadelphia, 41

31.   Louis C. Tiffany in 1880.

32.   Louis C. Tiffany, watercolor and pencil, *Flowers in Rome*,
February 1866. *Collection of Hugh F. McKean, Winter Park, Florida*

Valley of the Pines

March 2nd 66

33.   Louis C. Tiffany watercolor and pencil, *Valley of the Pines in Italy*, March 2, 1866. *Collection of Hugh F. McKean, Winter Park, Florida*

Rheims
July 16/89

Louis C. Tiffany

34.   Louis C. Tiffany, watercolor and pencil, *Rheims,* July 16, 1889. *Yale University Art Gallery. Gift of Louise Platt*

35.   Entry to Tiffany's Bella apartment studio from *Artistic Houses,* New York, 1882 (see color plate 2).

→

36.   Fireplace and overmantel in the Veterans Room of the Seventh Regiment
Armory decorated by Louis C. Tiffany in 1880.

37.   Studio in the Tiffany mansion at Seventy-second Street and Madison Avenue, constructed in 1885, demolished in 1936.

38. The fireplace in Tiffany's studio in the Tiffany mansion.

39. Louis C. Tiffany in 1886.

40.   Summer panel of the "Four Seasons" window designed by Louis C. Tiffany and displayed at the Paris Exposition in 1900. From 1904 until 1957 it was installed in Tiffany's Laurelton Hall. *Collection of Hugh F. McKean, Winter Park, Florida*

41.   Henri de Toulouse-Lautrec, "La Clownesse et les Cinq Plastrons" 1892, design for a window in the Philadelphia Museum of Art. *Gift of John D. McIlhenny* (see color plate 3)

→

42.   Tiffany glass window made from a design by Pierre Bonnard, exhibited in Paris in
1894, in the collection of S. Bing from 1895 until 1909. *Private collection, Paris*

43.   Tiffany windows at the Paris Exposition in 1900.

44. Mosaic of iridescent glass designed by Louis C. Tiffany, exhibited at the Paris Exposition in 1900. *Hessisches Landesmuseum, Darmstadt*

45. Louis C. Tiffany, watercolor rendering of the interior of the Lyceum Theatre, 1885. *The Metropolitan Museum of Art* →

46. Hanging light fixture designed by Louis C. Tiffany in 1885 for the Lyceum Theatre, formerly in the Havemeyer Collection. *University of Michigan, Ann Arbor*

47. Bronze and iridescent glass lamp with seven lights and prisms, Tiffany Studios, New York, circa 1900. →

48.   Wisteria tree lamp of coppered glass and bronze, Tiffany Studios, New York, circa 1905.

49.   Apple blossom tree lamp, Tiffany Studios, New York, circa 1905.

50. Eighteen-light electric lily lamp of glass and bronze designed by Louis C. Tiffany in 1902, Tiffany Studios, New York.

51. Pair of eight-light bronze lamps with blown-glass shades, Tiffany Studios, New York.

52. Lotus blossom lamp of coppered glass and bronze, Tiffany Studios, New York.

53. Watercolor design for a hanging dome shade for J. R. Martin, Bellevue Palace, Berne, Switzerland, approved by Louis C. Tiffany. *The Metropolitan Museum of Art. Gift of Julia Weld*

→

HANGING · DOME · SHADE ·
· MR · J · R · MARTIN ·
· BELLEVUE · PALACE ·
· BERN · SWITZERLAND ·

APPROVED

Louis C. Tiffany

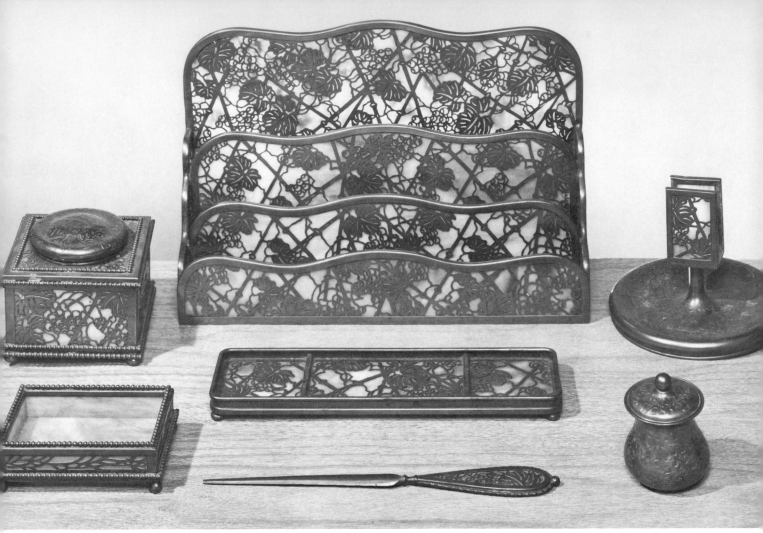

54. Etched metal and glass desk set, grapevine pattern by Tiffany Studios. *Victoria and Albert Museum, London*

55. Pair of bronze candlesticks by
Tiffany Studios. *Author's collection*

56–58.   Three photographs of the furnaces of Tiffany Studios showing the making of Tiffany glass in progress.

56.   A press for making tiles and jewels.

57.   Cleaning a glory hole.

58.   Jimmy Stewart's shop at work.

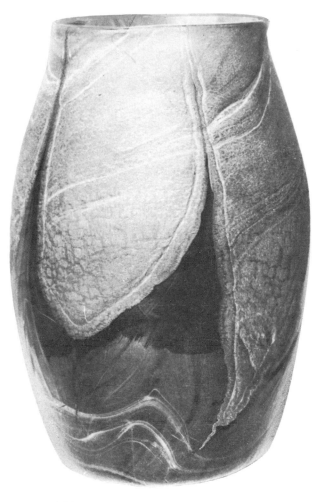

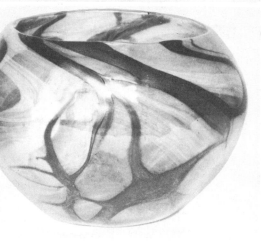

upper right:
59.   Bowl of green glass decorated with applied gold glass threads. Purchased from S. Bing, June 2, 1894. H.16 cm. *Collection of the Musée des Arts Décoratifs, Paris*

left:
60.   Ovoid vase of brown glass with veins of blue and black partially covered by a metallic glass envelope in the shape of four large irregular teeth. Purchased from S. Bing in 1895. H.18 cm. *Collection of the Musée des Arts Décoratifs, Paris*

lower right:
61.   Spheroid bowl of yellow glass with veins of white and blue black. Purchased from S. Bing in 1895. H.9 cm. *Collection of the Musée des Arts Décoratifs, Paris*

62.   Marbelized bottle-shaped vase of transparent mahogany-colored glass veined with red, green, blue, and brown, sometimes called "laminated glass." The original label on this vase reads "FABRILE" which was only used in 1892. H.14.5 cm. *Collection of the Metropolitan Museum of Art. Gift of H. O. Havemeyer, 1896*

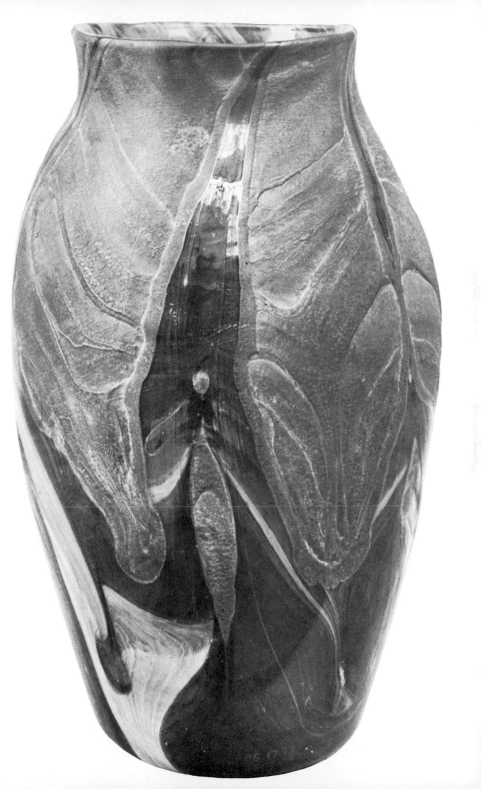

63. Opaque vase of brown and green glass with a striated surface imitating bronze similar to fig. 60. H. 22 cm. *Collection of the Metropolitan Museum of Art. Gift of H. O. Havemeyer, 1896*

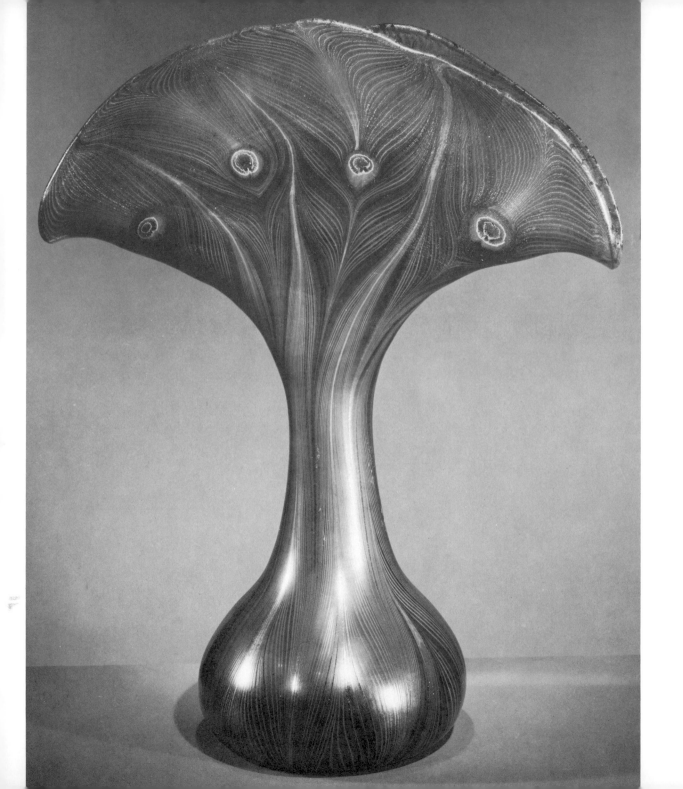

opposite page:

64. Peacock glass vase of iridescent blues and greens with feather and eye decorations. H.36 cm. *Collection of the Metropolitan Museum of Art. Gift of H. O. Havemeyer, 1896*

65. Iridescent bottle-shaped vase with fused leaf and vine decoration. *Collection of the Metropolitan Museum of Art. Gift of H. O. Havemeyer, 1896*

←

66. Iridescent glass plaque with
abstract floral decoration. *Collection of
the Metropolitan Museum of Art. Gift of
H. O. Havemeyer, 1896*

67. Glass lampshade mounted in a
metal stand for use with candles. The
glass is green and brown worked into
a free abstract design. H. 37 cm.
*Collection of the Metropolitan Museum of
Art. Gift of H. O. Havemeyer, 1896*

→

68–80. Thirty-nine vases and bowls acquired between 1894 and 1896 by the Smithsonian Institution in Washington, D.C., from the Tiffany Glass and Decorating Company. All are identified as "Favrile glass."

68. Double gourd-shaped vase of amber glass decorated with striped designs of blue, gray, and red in a leaf pattern with an iridescent surface. H. 30.4 cm.

69. Vase of light-green iridescent glass with dark-green and brown decoration. H.26.9 cm. With its original cover (fig. 78, no. 1) it appeared as frontispiece for *Tiffany Favrile Glass*, published in 1896. H. with cover 49.5 cm.

←

70. Vase of clouded white glass with a bluish-yellow iridescent effect. It has 21 narrow flat sides. H.33.9 cm.

71. Jardiniere bowl of green glass treated with a variety of iridescent colors. H.20.9 cm. →

72. (*far left*): Vase of common green bottle glass wound with a spiral glass thread and coated with an iridescence that changes from a deep blue green to a red purple according to the light. H.33 cm.

73. Vase of green glass mixed with brown and blue of a bulbous shape on top and bottom decorated with reddish-brown and blue seaweed-shaped leaves and an iridescent covering. H.45.7 cm.

74. Double gourd-shaped vase of brown glass covered with black, iridescent with irregular decoration. H.49.8 cm.

75. Vase of green glass covered with a deep blue and green iridescent effect. H.43.1 cm. →

76. (*from left to right*): 1. Bowl of amber glass with a mirrorlike coating of blue clouded with smoky yellow and highly iridescent. H.8.8 cm. 2. Vase of amber glass bent into an irregular bulbous triangle and decorated with broad leaves in varying shades of iridescent metallic blue. H.15.2 cm. 3. Amber glass vase, pear shaped, clouded with a greenish yellow and decorated with five branches of striated coarse leaves and an iridescent surface. H.15.8 cm.

77. 1. Vase with a trefoil top of iridescent blue-green glass with irregularly applied decoration of metallic glass shaded from silver to purple violet. 2. Vase or jar of yellow or amber glass with transparent waved lines around the body like brown seaweeds and then the outer surface is somewhat deadened. H.17.4 cm. 3. Bowl made of mixed opaque brown shades of red- and cream-colored glasses appearing like banded agate. H.11.4 cm.

78. (*opposite page, top row, from left to right*): 1. Cover for the vase or jar of fig. 69. 2. Bowl of amber glass streaked with yellowish gray and overlaid with streakings of opaque lava brown glass. H.9.5 cm. 3. Vase in a gilt wire stand, vase of amber glass with

a silvered coating at the top shading to a fiery purple at the bottom. H.12.7 cm. with stand 14.6 cm. 4. Vase of dark brown opaque glass streaked with brick red. H.10.4 cm. 5. Vase of dark opaque glass covered with red glass streaked with a brighter red and black. H.5.3 cm.

(*bottom row, from left to right*): 1. Bottle of opaque smoky yellow glass streaked with gray over which are drawn green leaves and stems in bright changeable iridescent colors. The sides have been pressed in, forming five large dimples. H.12 cm. 2. Bottle of dark opaque glass decorated with designs formed of yellow and silver lines, "something like the leaves of the wild turnip," on a ground of dark metallic luster. H.10.1 cm. 3. Vase in a bronze stand; vase made of mixed translucent and opaque glass veined with a creamy white and red brown. This was also illustrated in *Tiffany Favrile Glass*, 1896. H.20.9 cm., with its stand 26.6 cm. 4. Vase of green glass almost covered with clouds of bluish purple and drab. H.11.7 cm. 5. Vase of white glass over which is spread a dark brown and a bluish gray streaked with smoky yellow and with splashes of opaque lavalike glass from the lip down on the shoulder. H.12.7 cm.

79. (*from left to right*): 1. Bottle of white crystal glass with the outer surface ground or etched. Decorated with three tearlike patches of thick yellow glass between which are three plantlike designs of yellow becoming brown at their converging point. H.8.2 cm. 2. Vase composed of three layers of opaque glass, a green, a yellow, and a dark lava brown. It is decorated by cutting designs through the outer or lower coating showing mostly the yellow. In some cases, particularly in the lower part of the vase, the yellow has been cut through showing the green. H.13.9 cm. 3. Bowl of glass. The upper part is yellowish shading to blue below. The sides have mushroom-shaped figures in green shaded to brown. H.7.3 cm. 4. Vase presented as a gift to the Smithsonian Institution by

Charles L. Tiffany in 1896 is made of green glass decorated with fish, water lines, and scrollwork. The outlines of the fish, scales, and fins are cut by the lapidary's wheel to enhance the effect of the glass marquetry with intaglio carving. H.18 cm. 5. Bowl on a low foot made of opaque black and dark brown glass veined with blue, purple, and yellowish gray. It is decorated near the lip with threads of aventurine glass. H.11.1 cm. 6. Vase made of opaque glass shading from dark brown at the top through a green, reddish brown, and a yellow to a green at the base. H.13.9 cm. 7. Bottle made of a striated dark amber glass. H.12.3 cm.

80.   (*top row, from left to right*): 1. Vase of green and a creamy-gray glass. The upper part of the body has 16 sides. H.13.3 cm. 2. Vase of brown glass decorated with spiral bands of smoky drab, yellow, and bluish gray, also vertical double bands of yellow, changing to brown with green spots. H.12.7 cm. 3. Vase of brown glass covered with yellow and smoky gray. Six knobs are formed on the shoulder. Decorated with black and gray lines, "like the leaves of the wild turnip." H.18.4 cm. 4. Bottle of a yellowish-green glass covered with an iridescent film, indented in 5 places on the shoulder. H.18.7 cm.

(*bottom row, from left to right*): 1. Vase of green-tinted glass, the upper part covered with a thin metallic blue. Decorated from top to bottom with five groups of yellow lines and over all a changeable iridescent coating. H.17.7 cm. 2. Bottle of clouded amber glass shading through yellow to a smoky agate at the bottom. H.14.2 cm. 3. Bottle of an opaque pearly-gray glass over which are splashings of smoky yellow with changeable iridescent colors. H.24.1 cm. 4. Vase of blue glass decorated with vertical stripes like grass leaves with an iridescent surface. H.27.3 cm. 5. Vase of glass with an iridescent surface that gives the appearance of streams of liquid running and spreading out in a puddle. H.20.3 cm.

81.   Vase of colorless glass decorated with brown-speckled glass in an irregular pattern and a gold iridescent surface overall. Inscribed "L. C. T." H.10 cm. *Collection of the Hessisches Landesmuseum, Darmstadt*

82. Vase of rust-red glass with gold iridescent decoration in irregular abstract nature-inspired linear designs. Inscribed "L. C. T. E1986." H.15.6 cm. *Collection of the Hessisches Landesmuseum, Darmstadt*

83.   Ten-sided vase of dark-blue glass shading to violet brown with silver and gold iridescent glass decoration in undulating horizontal wavy stripes and light-yellow swirls. The rim consists of dark violet and dark olive-green colors. Inscribed "09909" H.23.5 cm. *Collection of the Hessisches Landesmuseum, Darmstadt*

84. Spherical vase of white opalescent glass with light brown vertical veins that show as red with interior lighting. The decoration is light green and violet leaf forms overlaid, combed, and rolled into the body. Marked "Tiffany Favrile Glass." Purchased from S. Bing, Paris, in 1896. II.11.5 cm. *Collection of the Museum für Kunst und Gewerbe, Hamburg*

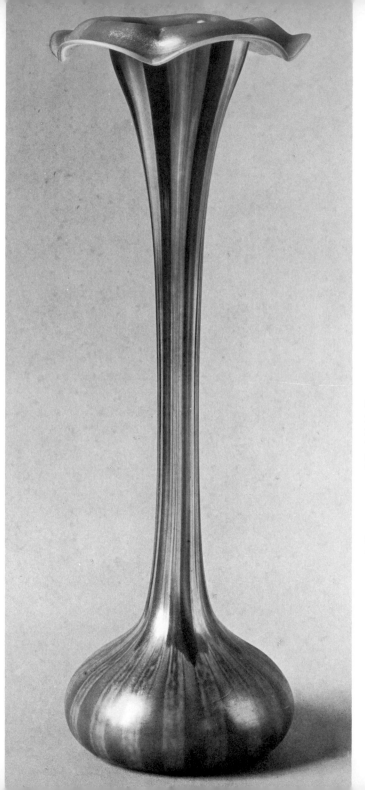

85. Onion-shaped vase with a long narrow neck that opens to five petals made of colorless opalescent glass with opaque brown and green vertical ribs. The opening is coated with a bright gold iridescence while the remaining exterior surface is lightly iridized. Marked "L. C. Tiffany Favrile," purchased through S. Bing from the Paris Exposition, 1900. H. 34.7 cm. *Collection of the Museum für Kunst und Gewerbe, Hamburg*

86. Double gourd-shaped vase of tomato-red opaque glass decorated with gold and purple swirls and an iridescent surface. Inscribed "Louis C. Tiffany E1895." Purchased through S. Bing from the Paris Exposition, 1900. H.26 cm. *Collection of the Museum für Kunst und Gewerbe, Hamburg*

87. The display of Tiffany Favrile Glass at the Paris Exposition in 1900.

88. Vase of Cypriote and gold iridescent glass. The rough textured Cypriote glass is applied and fused in five petal-shaped areas. Inscribed "Louis C. Tiffany K248." H.14.5 cm. Acquired from the Paris Exposition, 1900. *Collection of the Kunstgewerbemuseum, Berlin*

→

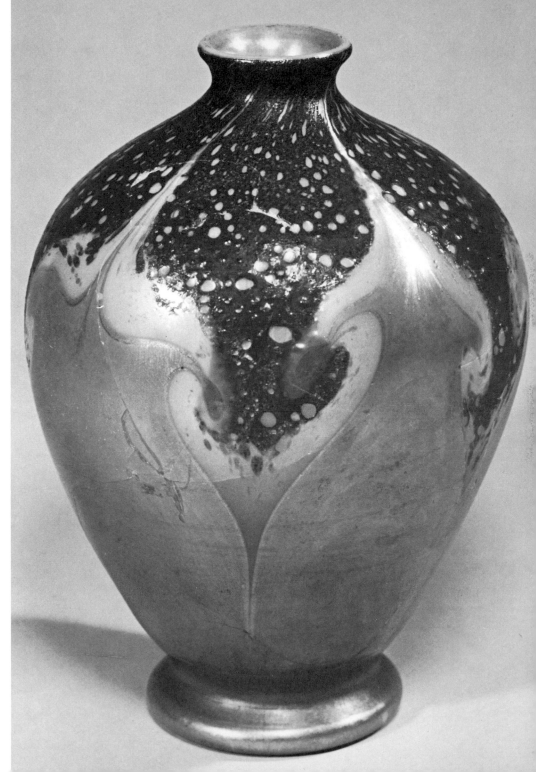

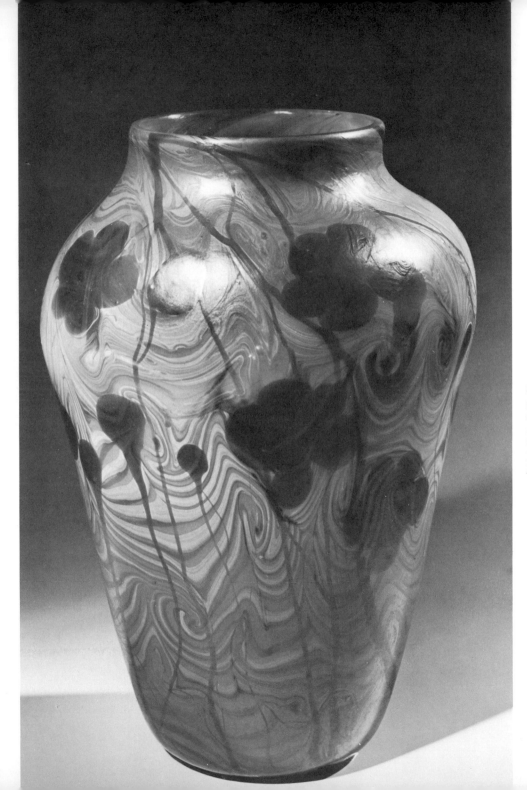

89.   Vase of red-yellow iridescent glass decorated with spiral swirls and applied dark purple flowers, leaves, and stems. Inscribed "Louis C. Tiffany 09155." H.38 cm. Acquired from the Paris Exposition, 1900. *Collection of the Kunstgewerbemuseum, Berlin*

90. Iridescent Tiffany glass and silver-plated bronze paperweight, wave design circa 1900. II.8 cm. *Author's collection*

91. Large gold iridescent glass vase decorated with fused lily-pad and random thread design, inscribed "Louis C. Tiffany 04552." H.58 cm. *Author's collection*

92. Base of a Tiffany glass bowl showing paper label used from 1893 until 1902. Glass inscribed "LCT A1513." *Private collection*

TRADE-MARK.

No. 42,012.   REGISTERED FEB. 9, 1904.

TIFFANY FURNACES.
DECORATIVE GLASSWARE.
APPLICATION FILED MAY 29, 1903.

FAVRILE

Witnesses: Proprietor.

93.   Tiffany trademark in use from 1902 until 1919.

94. Detail of fig. 95 showing the inscription.

95. Tiffany vase. *Collection of the
Museum of Fine Arts, Boston. Gift of
J. Jonathan Joseph*

96. Tiffany crystal and colored glass vase with intaglio-carved decoration. *Collection of the Walters Art Gallery, Baltimore, Maryland*

97.   Four Tiffany vases from the A. Douglas Nash Collection. Now at the
Carnegie Institute, Pittsburgh, Pennsylvania.
(*from left to right*:)

   1. Exhibition piece, purple iridescent with green leaf and vine decoration,
   inscribed "Louis C. Tiffany–Favrile 9661A," exhibited in St. Louis 1904 and in
   Paris 1906. 19.5 cm.

   2. Vase with inserted glass jewels, purple iridescent glass, inscribed "L. C.
   Tiffany–Favrile 3532P." H.15.2 cm.

   3. Vase with intaglio carved decoration. 24 cm.

   4. Morning glory vase, paperweight technique, inscribed "L. C. Tiffany–
   Favrile 3309J," exhibited in 1914. H.16.5 cm.

98.   Six Tiffany glass vases and bowls. *Collection of the Museum of Modern Art,
New York. Gift of Joseph H. Heil*

→

99.   Tiffany glass vase with millefiori canes and floral decoration in varying shades of blues and greens, iridescent surface, H.34 cm. *Collection of the Museum of Modern Art, Edgar Kaufmann, Jr., Fund*

100.   Tiffany iridescent glass vase in three shades of blue from silvery to dark decorated with an abstract floral design. H. 32 cm. *Collection of the Museum of Modern Art, Edgar Kaufmann, Jr., Fund*

101. Tiffany vase with a swirl design in grays and blues of iridescent glass on a red glass body. Inscribed "04536." H.27 cm. *Collection of the Museum of Modern Art, Phyllis B. Lambert Fund*

102. Small Tiffany glass vase with a
flowing floral design of gray on a
matte black body with a blue iridescent
interior. Inscribed "R199." H.11.5 cm.
*Collection of the Museum of Modern Art,
Phyllis B. Lambert Fund*

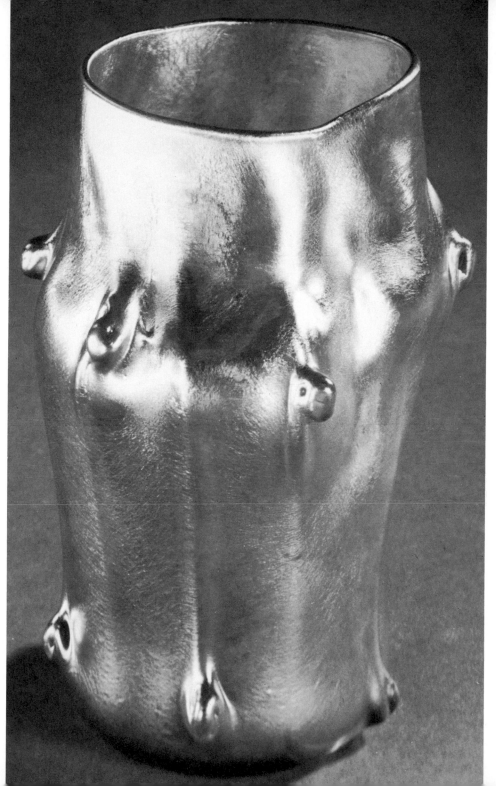

103.   Small Tiffany lava glass bowl of blue and gold iridescent glass. Inscribed "155P." H.9.5 cm. *Collection of the Museum of Modern Art, Phyllis B. Lambert Fund*

104.   Gold iridescent glass vase of irregular shape with wartlike knobs. Inscribed "L. C. Tiffany–Favrile 6159D." H.15 cm. *Collection of the Museum of Modern Art, New York*

105. Two Cypriote vases and one paperweight technique Tiffany glass vase. The largest, with abstract designs imbedded in clear glass, is 30 cm. in height. *Collection of the Museum of Modern Art, New York*

106. Two flower-form vases and one lava glass vase of varicolored Tiffany glass. The small lava vase was included in the 1946 sale of Tiffany's private collection. *Collection of the Museum of Modern Art, New York*

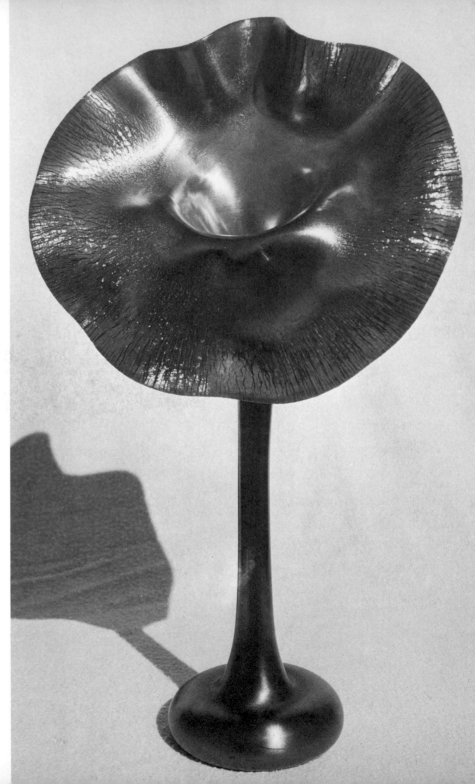

107.   Blue iridescent "jack-in-the-pulpit" Tiffany glass vase with purple and green luster. Inscribed "9557G." H. 45 cm. *Collection of the Corning Museum of Glass*

108. Vase of light blue and green
opalescent glass with an iridescent
lining both cameo- and intaglio-carved
to resemble a giant opal. Inscribed
"L. C. Tiffany–Favrile 275D." H.27 cm.
Author's collection.

109. Two Tiffany glass vases, one with brown and tan linear
decorations fused into a gourd-shaped body of dark-blue
iridescent glass. H.32.7 cm. The other has dark green and brown
decorations in a pale transparent green iridescent glass body.
H.39.3 cm. *Collection of the Victoria and Albert Museum, London*

110.   Four examples of Tiffany glass—a vase, a rosewater sprinkler, a bowl, and a bottle.
The gooseneck sprinkler vase is of peacock glass. H.36.8 cm. *Collection of the Victoria and
Albert Museum, London*

111.   A plaque of Tiffany peacock glass in green, blue, and brown iridescent colors. D.23.1 cm. Also a vase combining peacock eyes with Cypriote glass texture. H.25 cm. *Collection of the Victoria and Albert Museum, Bethnal Green Branch, London*

112.   Large Tiffany glass vase of dark blue, green, and yellow iridescent marbelized swirl pattern later called "King Tut" when produced by the Durand Art Glass Works. H.49.2 cm. *Collection of the Victoria and Albert Museum, Bethnal Green Branch, London*

113.   Four Tiffany vases (*left to right*): 1. Vase of orange glass with silver color vine and leaf decoration. 2. Vase of irregular shaped Cypriote glass. 3. Vase of varying shades of iridescent blue using the blow-out technique. Vase was acquired at the Paris Exposition in 1900. 4. Vase decorated with a design similar to no. 1 but darker in color. All H. between 10.7 cm and 13.9 cm. *Collection of the Victoria and Albert Museum, London*

114.   Entrance to Louis C. Tiffany's Laurelton Hall, designed and decorated by Louis C. Tiffany between 1902 and 1905, demolished in 1957.

115.   Interior of an alcove of the living room of Louis C. Tiffany's Laurelton Hall showing the installation of his stained-glass windows.

→

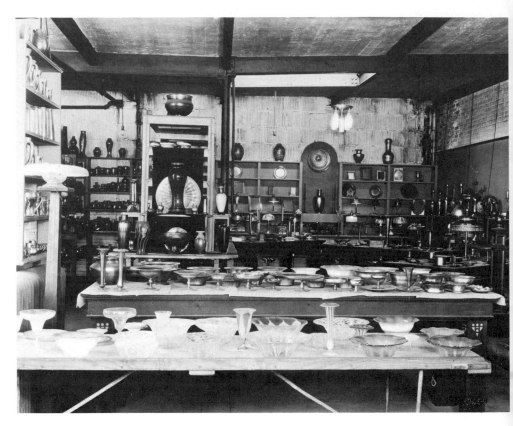

116.   Display area and storeroom of Tiffany Furnaces in Corona, New York, before 1928.

117.   Peacock necklace of gold and amethysts, opals, sapphires, rubies, pearls, emeralds, demantoids, and topazes designed by Louis C. Tiffany, made by Julia Sherman, exhibited in St. Louis 1904 and Paris 1906. Marked "Tiffany & Co." Length open 25.5 cm. *Collection of Hugh and Jeanette McKean, Winter Park, Florida* →

118. Necklace of gold, opals, and enamel. Pendant with large oval opal surrounded by grape leaves in green enamel and grapes formed of circular opals set in gold. Marked "Tiffany & Co." Length open 45 cm. *Collection of the Metropolitan Museum of Art*

119. Necklace of gold, turquoise, and enamel. Marked "Tiffany & Co." *Collection of Gladys L. Koch*

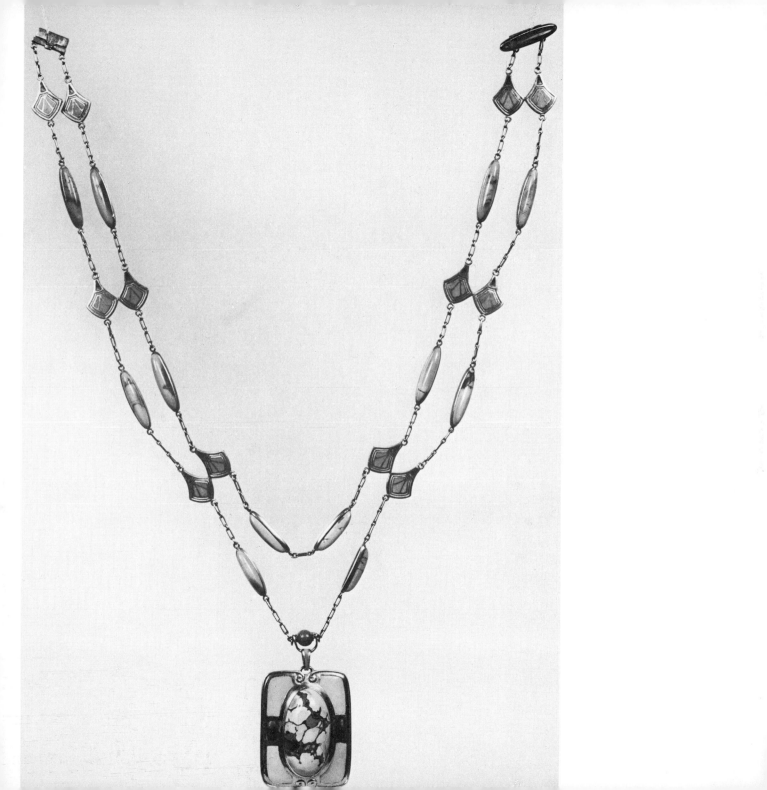

120. Fireplace set with sample Tiffany glass tiles installed in Tiffany Studio showrooms and used to display Tiffany glass.

121. Opaque glass vase with varicolored bits of broken glass partially fused into a ground of red, yellow, and green to resemble a mosaic, then decorated with a pattern of whitish green vines and flowers, iridescent over all. Inscribed "L. C. T. E2097" H.18.1 cm. *Collection of the Kunstmuseum, Düsseldorf. Gift of Helmut Hentrich*

122.   Vase of colorless opalescent glass with varicolored inlays of millefiori flowers with blue-white petals and green leaves in a paperweight technique. The interior has a delicate iridescence. Inscribed "8150D L. C. Tiffany–Favrile" H.14.3 cm. *Collection of the Kunstmuseum, Düsseldorf. Gift of Helmut Hentrich*

123.   Bowl of clear glass embodying
ten overlapping petals of colored glass
shading from opal white to blue violet.
Five alternate petals are cut and
polished to appear as cameos on the
outer surface. Marked "163 A–Coll.
L. C. Tiffany–Favrile." H.7.5 cm. *Collection of the Kunstmuseum, Düsseldorf.
Gift of Helmut Hentrich*

124.   Tiffany glass bowl, paperweight technique glass with iridescent lining.
Inscribed "Louis C. Tiffany R.2415." H.21.5 cm. *Collection of the Metropolitan Museum of Art. Gift of the Louis Comfort Tiffany Foundation, 1951*

125.   Bowl of dark blue and gold iridescent glass, "lava" type. Inscribed "L. C. Tiffany–Favrile 21 A–Coll." H.16 cm. *Collection of the Metropolitan Museum of Art. Gift of the Louis Comfort Tiffany Foundation, 1951*

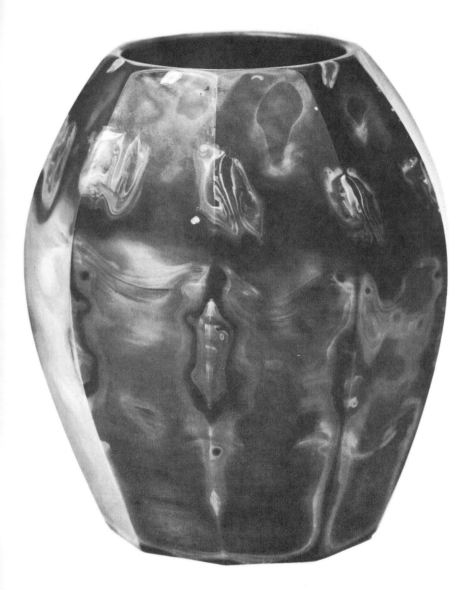

126. Ten-sided cut and polished agate glass vase, marbelized glass of green, yellow, brown, and tan. Inscribed "L. C. Tiffany–Favrile Salon 1906 105 A–Coll." H.10 cm. *Collection of the Metropolitan Museum of Art. Gift of the Louis Comfort Tiffany Foundation, 1951*

127. Morning-glory vase, paperweight technique glass with iridescent lining, blues and greens in clear glass. Inscribed "L. C. Tiffany–Favrile 150 A–Coll." H.17 cm. *Collection of the Metropolitan Museum of Art. Gift of the Louis Comfort Tiffany Foundation, 1951* →

128. Photograph of Louis C. Tiffany relaxing in the gardens of his home in Laurelton Hall, Oyster Bay, New York, after his retirement in 1919.

Index

A

Abstract Expressionism, 1, 33
agate glass, 22
Amaya, Mario, 1, 33
annealing process, 12, 20
anticlassical naturalism, 1
antique glass, 16
Antiques, 24
aquamarine glass, 20–21, 22; making of, 20
Art de Décoration, 19
Arthur, Chester (President), 4
Artistic Japan, 4
Art Nouveau, 1–2; applied to objects, 19, 24; and avant-garde painting of the period, 33; decline in popularity of, 26; revival during mid-1950s, 30; Tiffany as leading American artist of, 3–5, 7–8
Ascot (pattern), 25
aventurine glass, 11

B

Bach, Martin, 9, 19
Barrows, George S., 30
basketwork glass, 23
beauty, Tiffany's definition of, 35. *See* "Quest of Beauty, The"
"Bella" apartment, 1, 4
Bing, Samuel, 8, 13, 18, 43; appreciation of Tiffany's art, 1–2, 4; death of, 27; and the *Salon de l'Art Nouveau*, 10, 29. *See also* "Louis C. Tiffany's Coloured Glass Work" (Bing)
Blake, William, influence on Tiffany, 4
blown glass, 5, 7, 9, 10; decoration of, 11; globes, 40; lampshades, 7, 25, 40, Ill. 50; making of, 11, 20; numbering of, 13; as Tiffany's highest achievement, 1–2; vases, 19
blowout glass, 22
Bonnard, Pierre, 43; window designed by, Ill. 42
bowls, 12; Favrile, Ill. 123; jardiniere, Ill. 71; lava glass, Ills. 22, 103, 125; paperweight technique, Ill. 124

Briggs, Joseph, 29
bronze works, 7

C

cameo carved glass, 22
candlesticks, 7, 30, Ill. 55; numbering of, 7
chintz glass, 23
Christ Church, 37
Chrysler, Walter P., Jr., 30
Chrysler Museum, 30
Cincinnati Museum of Art, 10, 29
classicism, 33
Coats, James, 30
Coleman, Samuel, 29
Collecting Tiffany products, 29–30
Collection of Louis C. Tiffany, 29
Colonial (pattern), 25
color: of glass, 19–20, 22, 25; importance of, 34; of jewelry, 26
"Color and Its Kinship to Sound" (Tiffany), 35–39
Columbian Exposition, 9
Connelly, Brian, 30
Cook, George J., 11
Corona factory, 19, 25
Corona Glass, 9
Corot, Jean Baptiste, 3
Craftsman, The, 20
crystal glass, 22
Cypriote glass, 11–12, 23

D

De Cesnold, General, 11
De Goncourt brothers, 29
desk sets, 8, 30, Ill. 54
diatreta glass, 23
Dominion (pattern), 25

E

Earl (pattern), 25
Edison, Thomas A., 7
Edward C. Moore Collection, 11

Edward Webb Glasshouse, 9
enamels, 25, 26, 40
Exposition of 1878 (Paris), 3
Exposition Universelle (1900, Paris), 4
expressionism, 33

F
"Fabrile," 10
"Favrile": derivation of name, 10; glass, 11, 15, 25–26,
    29, 33; lamps, 25; pottery, 25–26; trademark, 10, Ill. 93
"Favrile Beetle Jewelry," 26. *See also* jewelry
First World War, 7, 26
Flemish (pattern), 25
"Four Seasons" (window), 5, Ill. 40

G
Gallé, Emile, 15, 33
Gillinder Brothers, 9
glass: registration of, 13. *See also* numbering
glassblowing, 9
glassmaking, Ills. 56–58
Grady, James H., 12
Grafton Galleries, 43
Great Depression, 1, 30

H
Havemeyer, Mr. and Mrs. Henry O., 10, 11, 29
Haworth Art Gallery, 30
Heil, Joseph, 30
Hentrich, Helmut, 31
Hollingsworth, John, 9, 19
hollow ware, 25–26
Hugh F. McKean Collection, 43

I
Inness, George, 3
intaglio carved glass, 23
International Style (Bauhaus-initiated), 30
iridescence, 11, 17, 19, 22; in blown glass, 4, 9–10; pro-
    cess of making, 16
Iris (pattern), 25

Islamic glass, 11

J
jack-in-the-pulpit vase, 19, Ill. 107
jeweled glass, 23
jewelry, 25, 26
Joseph, J. Jonathan, 31
Joseph Heil Collection, 30

K
Kandinsky, Wassily, 34
Kaufmann, Edgar, Jr., 30
Kemp, George, 3, 4; Tiffany's decoration of house of,
    4, 43
Klee, Paul, 34
Kunstmuseum, 31
Kunst und Kunsthandwerk (Bing), 13, 43

L
"La Clownesse et les Cinq Plastrons" (window), Ill. 41
La Farge, John, 4, 43
Lalique, 33
laminated glass, 23
lamps, 2, 8, 12, 14, 26, 34: bronze and glass, Ills. 4, 5, 47,
    48, 50, 51; first metal and glass, 7; first portable, 7
lampshades, leaded glass, 7, 8, 30
Laurelton Hall, 25, 29, 30; stained-glass windows at, Ill.
    115
lava glass, 11, 12, 23
"L. C. Tiffany Favrile" (trademark), 10
leaded glass, 10, 12; ceiling light, 29; panels, 3; window,
    Ill. 3; windowscreen, Ill. 2
lime glass, 12
Lobmeyer (Austrian firm of glassmakers), 4
Louis C. Tiffany Foundation, 25, 27, 30
"Louis C. Tiffany's Coloured Glass Work" (Bing), 13–18
Louis C. Tiffany's Glass—Bronzes—Lamps (Koch), 30
Louisiana Purchase Exposition, 26
Lounsbery, Elizabeth, 20, 44
Lyceum Theatre: decoration of, 4; Tiffany glass lighting
    device there, 7, Ill. 46

M

McIlhenny, Doctor Parker, 10
McKean, Hugh F., 30, 44
McKean Collection, 30
Manderson, Thomas, 9, 11, 19
Manderson, William, 9
Manhattan (pattern), 25
marks on Tiffany products, 24, 26; forged, 25
Metropolitan Museum of Art, 7, 10, 11, 19, 29
millefiori glass, 12, 21, 23; Grady's lily pad and vine decoration, 12
modernism, 1
"Modernists," 35
Monet, Claude, 12
Moore, Edward C., 11, 29
mosaic, 16, 30; designed by Tiffany, Ill. 44
Mount, Ward, 30
Munch, Edvard, 33
Murano, 17
Musée des Arts Décoratifs (Paris), 10
Museum of Fine Arts, 31
Museum of Modern Art, 30

N

Nabis, 33
Nash, A. Douglas, 12, 22
Nash, Arthur J., 9, 29
National Academy of Design, 3
Nature, Tiffany's view of, 37
necklace, Ills. 118, 119; peacock, Ill. 117
New York Times, The, 10
numbering: of candlesticks, 30; of desk set items, 30; of glass, 24

O

opalescent glass, 11, 16
Oriental art, influence on Tiffany, 29
overlay glass, 23

P

painting on glass, 15, 36–37

Pan-American Exposition (1901), 19
paperweight, glass and bronze, Ill. 90
paperweight technique, 12
paperweight-technique glass, 23
Paris International Exposition (1900), 7, 19; display of Tiffany Favrile Glass at, Ill. 87
Parker, George, 9
Partial List of Windows, A, 43
patterns. See hollow ware; individual entries
peacock glass, 17, 23; making of, 11
Peacock Necklace, 44
peacock's feather motif, 17
Philadelphia Centennial Exposition (1876), 9
plaque: iridescent glass, Ill. 66; peacock glass, Ill. 111
"pontil," 20
pottery, 26, 40
Prince (pattern), 25
punch bowl (at Paris Exposition of 1900), 19, Ill. 10

Q

Queen (pattern), 25
"Quest of Beauty, The" (Tiffany), 35
Quezal Art Glass Company, 19

R

reactive glass, 23
registry numbers by years (list), 40
Rembrandt Club, 35
Richardson, Henry H., 1
Roman glass, 11
Romantics, 37
Royal (pattern), 25

S

Salon de l'Art Nouveau, 4, 10, 29
Salon du Champs de Mars, 4
Salon of 1905 (Paris), 44
Sandwich Glass Company, 9
Saunders, Arthur E., 12, 20
Savoy (pattern), 25
Schmutzler, Robert, 1, 3–4, 33

Scotia (steamship), 3
Second World War, 2, 30
signatures: on glass, 8, 24; on vase, Ill. 94. *See also* marks
  on Tiffany products
Smithsonian Institution, 10, 29
stained glass, 14, 35; making of, 15
Stewart, James, 10
Stourbridge Glass Company, The, 9
Sullivan, Louis, 1
Symbolists, 33

T
table glass, 22
Tiffany, Charles Lewis, 3, 13; death of, 25
Tiffany, Louis C., 5, 7, 8, 9, 10, 11, 19, 21, 24, 25, 26, 27;
  artistic beginnings of, 1, 3–4; as collector, 29, 40; death
  of, 5, 30; and decorative art, 13–18, 34; paintings by,
  Ills. 32, 33, 34, 45; photographs of, Ills. 31, 39, 128; re-
  tirement of, 22
Tiffany and Company, 3, 11, 22, 25, 26; shutdown of fac-
  tory in 1928, 27
"Tiffany Favrile Glass," 10
"Tiffany Favrile Pottery," 10
Tiffany Furnaces, 9, 12, 13, 19, 22, 26
Tiffany Glass and Decoration Company, 5, 9, 10, 29
Tiffany Glass Company, 5, 9
Tiffany mansion, construction of, 4
Tiffany revival, 2
Tiffany Studios, 5, 7, 8, 43; catalogs and price lists of, 30;
  furnaces, Ills. 56–58. *See also* Tiffany Glass and Decora-
  tion Company
tiles, 30, Ill. 120
Toulouse-Lautrec, Henri, 43; window design of "La
  Clownesse et les Cinq Plastrons," Ill. 41
Trademark: Favrile, 10, Ill. 93

U
Universal Exposition. See *Exposition Universelle*

V
Van Gogh, Vincent, 33
vases, 2, 10, 12, 17, 21, 30; agate, Ills. 24, 30, 126;
  aquamarine glass, 21, Ill. 28; blowout technique, Ill.
  113; cameo glass, Ill. 27; cameo-and-intaglio-carved,
  Ill. 108; copper, 26; Cypriote, Ills. 18, 29, 88, 105, 113;
  Favrile glass, 30, Ills. 20, 84, 85, 87, 97; flower-form, 9,
  Ill. 106; free-form, 34; with intaglio carving, Ills. 79, 96;
  jack-in-the-pulpit, 19, Ill. 107; "King Tut" (pattern), Ill.
  112; laminated glass, Ill. 62; lava glass, Ills. 19, 106;
  making of, 17; with millefiori canes, Ill. 99; miniature,
  Ill. 23; with mosaic effect, Ill. 121; numbering of, 12;
  paperweight, 21, Ills. 23, 24, 25; paperweight tech-
  nique, 12, Ills. 97, 105, 122, 127; peacock glass, Ills. 26,
  64, 110; tall stem, 9; from Tiffany furnaces, 12
Vedder, Elihu, 4
Venetian glassware, 15, 21
Verneuil, M., 19
Veterans Room of the Seventh Regiment Armory, 4
Victoria (pattern), 25

W
White, Stanford, 43; collaboration with Tiffany on Veterans Room of the Seventh Regiment Armory, 4
White House, decoration of, 4
Wilson, Frederick, 5
windows, 7, 11, 12, 14, 26, 34, 36–37, 43; church windows, 4, 5; collected, 5; "Four Seasons," Ill. 40; opalescent glass, 4; at *Exposition Universelle*, 4; at *Salon
  du Champs de Mars*, 4; at *Salon de l'Art Nouveau*, 4;
  stained-glass, 3, 4, 15, 16, 38
World's Fair, 7